Agile Government Contracting

Expert Guidance for Department, Command and Agency Leaders, Contracting Officers, Procurement Professionals, Program and Project Managers, and Prime Contractors and Sub-Contractors

John G. Stenbeck, PMP®, PMI-ACP®, CSM, CSP
Kevin M. Jans, CACM, former Contracting Officer

FIRST EDITION

Agile **Government Contracting**

Expert Guidance for Department, Command, and Agency Leaders, Contracting Officers, Procurement Professionals, Program and Project Managers, and Prime Contractors and Sub-Contractors

John G. Stenbeck, PMP®, PMI-ACP®, CSM, CSP
Kevin M. Jans, CFCM, former Contracting Officer

Published by:
GR8PM, Inc.
7918 El Cajon Blvd. #N-326
La Mesa, CA 91942 USA
(619) 890-5807
custserv@gr8pm.com; http://www.gr8pm.com/

1st edition.
Printed in the United State of America.

ISBN Edition: 978-0-9846693-4-9

Cover Art:
Tamara Parsons, Kensington Type & Graphics
http://www.kentype.com

John's Acknowledgements

A debt that cannot be repaid is owed to a great many professional friends who took time from their hectic schedules to help make this book better than we thought possible.

Michelle R. Brunswick, Congressional Appropriations Liaison for U.S. Air Force, U.S. House of Representatives, and contributing author of *Project Management Circa 2025, chapter 19, U.S. Defense Acquisition 2025,* not only took the time to review it and provide critical feedback but offered an unsolicited endorsement for which we are deeply grateful.

Four others made particularly significant contributions that affected the core structure of this book. To them we owe a special acknowledgement. They are:

- **Michael O'Brochta,** PMP, PMI-ACP, former Central Intelligence Agency Project Manager and President, Zozer, Inc.
- **Kevin Underwood,** Financial Analyst, Booz Allen Hamilton, CDC MISO – Information Management Support Services (IMSS) Team
- **Gary Rapp,** Retired Law Enforcement and Information Technology Manager
- **John Watson,** General Manager and Sr. Consultant, GR8PM, Inc.

Finally, five more went above and beyond in helping and encouraging me, and to them I also owe a special thank you! They are:

- **Stanley E. Johnson,** MBA, PMP, CSM, IIS Manager Enabling (C2/C4ISR/EW), New Zealand Defence Force
- **Norman Anthony Aiello,** PMP
- **Dave Cunningham**
- **Adam Curtis**
- **Phil Hertzig**

In addition it was our pleasure to work on this second book project with Lauren Mix, our tireless and insightful editor, and Tamara Parsons, a creative graphic design genius. Without their vital input you want to read the content or even look at this book ... and it never would have been finished anyway!

Last but not least, thanks, as always, to our Operations Manager, J.T. Stenbeck, and our Office Manager, Lindsey Commuso, for keeping things running at GR8PM so I could write this book!

Kevin's Acknowledgements

Thank you seems insufficient for all the people who have helped craft the underlying experience which helped me add the contracting officer's perspective to this book. There are so many whose support, patience and belief in me helped create who, where and what I am today, which now includes being a published author. Thank you all for that. This book is for you.

There are also a few people whose direct involvement in, or in support of, this book made it happen.

Thanks to the entire Skyway team for keeping our great company charging ahead while I took time to work with John. Jim Licata, Lisa McMenamin, and Vicky Strycharske did some particularly heavy lifting for us. Thank you.

Finally, thanks to Shelley Hall for her significant contributions to the book. Shelley provided a great deal of experience and insights to the contracting section. Between the two of us, we have over a half-century of experience as Government contracting personnel. I hope it shows in this book.

Key Contributor

Shelley A. Hall has served as a Contracting Officer (with an Unlimited Warrant), a Procurement Analyst, and a Supervisory Contract Specialist across two Major Air Force Commands. She has over 31 years of experience that includes a variety of acquisitions and programs, including supplies and services, commercial and non-commercial, small purchases and major aircraft acquisitions, contracting and acquisition policy, and foreign military sales. Therefore, she really knows Government contracting

Dedication

JOHN STENBECK: To my sons, JT and Michael, who inspire and motivate me!

To my Saturday morning Men's Group and my Cursillo brothers who always cheer me on... please keep praying for me!

KEVIN JANS: To my wife Holly, for her steadfast support and patience while I hammer away at the keyboard through many long nights building our company – and writing books like this one.

To my kids, Mallory and Mitch, who give me the inspiration to dream, the time to focus, and the energy to create.

About the Authors

John G. Stenbeck, PMP, PMI-ACP, CSM, CSP, is the President of GR8PM, Inc.GR8PM, Inc. (pronounced "Great PM") and author of ***"PMI-ACP® and Certified Scrum Professional Exam Prep and Desk Reference"*** which has achieved over $1 million in sales.

He has the ability to manage large, complex projects to success because of his combined background in Accounting, Operations and I.T. His deep expertise has been applied to implementing enterprise resource planning (E.R.P.) systems as a client-side project manager for businesses with engineer-to-order (ETO) or configure-to-order (CTO) operations. His expertise in applying the FARs and DFARs and command of EVM for DCAA and DCMAO audits is of particular interest to many clients.

John is an Adjunct Instructor for the University of California teaching in the Systems Engineering Certificate program. He has taught numerous public and corporate on-site programs to over 9,000 students.

A partial list of John's clients includes: Booz Allen Hamilton, Inc. – Defense Information Technologies Group, McLean, VA; U.S. Army – Space and Terrestrial Communications Directorate, Fort Monmouth, NJ; and U.S.D.A. – National Finance Center, New Orleans, LA.

John is certified by PMI as a Project Management Professional (PMP®) and an Agile Certified Practitioner (PMI-ACP®). He also holds Certified Scrum Master (CSM) and Certified Scrum Professional (CSP) designations from the Scrum Alliance and an Information Technology Infrastructure Library (ITIL) v3 Foundations certification. He graduated from San Diego State University with a B.S. Business Administration, emphasis in Accounting.

Kevin M. Jans is the President of Skyway Acquisition Solutions, LLC. After spending 16 years as a DoD contracting officer, he founded Skyway to help small but sophisticated companies navigate the Federal market. Kevin leads a team of former COs from a variety of agencies and departments.

Kevin has been a CO in multiple DoD agencies, awarding hundreds of contracts valued from $7,700 to $882 million. He has also managed nearly four-dozen competitive Government source selections from aircraft and space systems to facilities and tactical vehicles to technical and knowledge-based services.

His "super power" is the ability to break the complex competitive source selection process into clear, actionable processes. Skyway's clients include dozens of companies in a variety of industries. To see some of these clients, visit www.skywayacquisition.com/testimonials.

Kevin also has elite training experience in DOD contracting through the Air Force's Copper Cap Training and Contracting Career Broadener Programs. He is a Certified Federal Contracts Manager through the National Contract Management Association (NCMA), and he is DOD-Certified in both Contracting and Program Management through Defense Acquisition University (DAU). He also presents frequently on the Government market and source selections for NCMA.

Table of Contents

CHAPTER

1

Introduction

At the highest level, Government contracting and Project Management share in common two approaches – ***Traditional*** and ***Agile.***

For many years, the Government has been trying to adopt and adapt Agile practices because the ***Clinger-Cohen Act*** (Pub. L No. 104-106, 1996) made it ***mandatory***. However, making that transition has proven difficult!

There are a number of issues making this transition difficult. One of the critical problems has been a lack of good information on how Government personnel can use Agile methods ***legally!*** Another has been an ever-increasing workload for Government personnel, eliminating any time for researching and analyzing the deepening labyrinth of Government regulations to identify specific procedures for applying Agile.

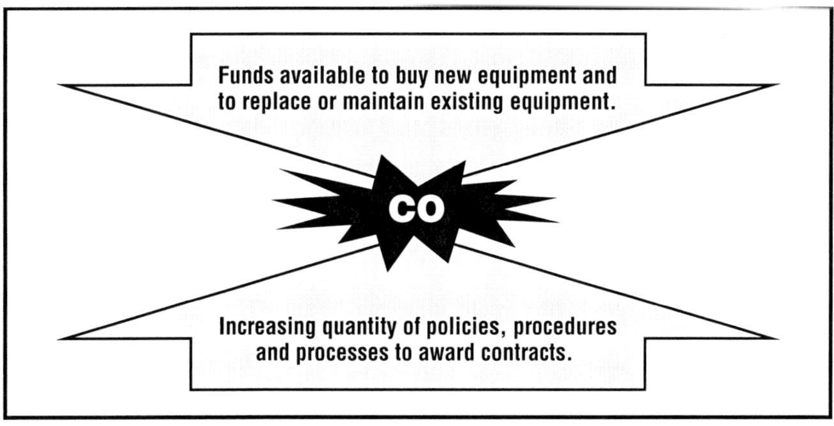

Figure 1.1 – Constraints impacting CO decision making.

In some cases, the actual workload (as defined by number of contracts and funds to obligate) is decreasing due to dwindling funds. However, the timelines to award these contracts and fill these requirements are getting longer because the volume of mandatory processes and documentation is increasing. In other words, the customer, the Program Manger, the Contracting Officer (CO), and even the taxpayer is spending more and getting less. This book provides specific examples and recommendations on how to use Agile strategies to reverse, or at least decrease, that trend.

The challenge for Government acquisition teams has always been to simplify the complex. The ***simplicity*** lies in judiciously spending taxpayer dollars to purchase needed goods and services. The ***complexity*** lies in doing so within the inter-related elements of the U.S. Constitution, the United States Code (U.S.C), Federal Acquisition Regulations (FAR), Federal Management Regulations (FMR), the policies of the agency or department, and even Presidential Executive Orders.

In many ways, the situation for Government contracting reflects the quote attributed to famous jurist Oliver Wendell Holmes Jr. (1841 -1935), who said, "I would not give a fig for the simplicity this side of complexity, but I would give my life for the simplicity on the other side of complexity."

To provide an understanding of the standard a CO must meet, it is helpful to review the regulatory guidance on the Contracting Officer's authority. ***FAR Part 1.602-1(b)*** requires the CO *"ensures that all requirements of law, executive orders, regulations, and all other applicable procedures, including clearances and approvals, have been met"* before they sign any Government contract. Read that italicized text one more time. Think about the far-reaching scope of that standard and see how easy it is for Government contracting to be seen as un-Agile or even anti-Agile!

The good news is that the next paragraph of the FAR ***(FAR 1.602-2)*** balances that extraordinary level of responsibility with the following, "In order to perform these responsibilities, contracting officers should be allowed wide latitude to exercise business judgment." That judgment allows the CO to implement Agile processes and tools. It also enables contracting and program management leaders to embrace these Agile processes to save time and resources.

This book solves those problems with ***specific, step-by-step procedural outlines*** backed by dozens of citations from the relevant regulations, ***saving hundreds of hours*** of research and analysis in order to properly negotiate, plan and deliver desirable outcomes using Agile methods on acquisitions of all sizes.

This book contains ***Agile-specific citations*** from the Federal Acquisition Regulations (FAR), the Defense FAR Supplement (DFARS), Federal Office of Management and Budget (OMB) Circulars, Federal Executive Orders, and Congressional Legislative Mandates.

For Department, Command and Agency leaders, Traditional methods have a long track record of ***legal reliability.*** Unfortunately, many decades of experience also show that Traditional methods have varying levels of success appearing to have a strong inverse correlation to complexity and uncertainty. In other words, the higher the complexity and uncertainty, the lower the probability of success. One of our goals is to "simplify the complex" because history has shown that in Government contracting, complexity and success are often off-setting.

In contrast, some Agile methods are new, and without the specific guidance in this book, may be legally risky, but they deliver reliable results with the best cost/schedule/performance profile in procurements that have high complexity and uncertainty. They also fulfill the ***Clinger-Cohen Act mandate. (Pub. L No. 104-106, 1996)***

It will be a challenge moving Government acquisitions from Traditional ***prescriptive*** processes, with detailed specifications, to ***discovery*** processes, with iterative and adaptive methods, because organizations and people must change. They must also embrace the concept of evolution. The Traditional model assumes the acquisition strategies that worked before will always work again. That assumption may be flawed.

For example, the acquisition strategy for a $1 billion, multiple award agency-wide contract for knowledge management services that worked in 2008 is not going to be as effective in 2014. Why? For starters, the economy was in free-fall in 2008 and many people were looking for work. Compare that with 2014. The economy has recovered much of its momentum, unemployment is under 7% again, and payrolls have also officially topped the 2008 levels. People with specialized knowledge of earned value management, engineering, program management, cost estimating and the like are now, once again, in demand in the commercial market. There are many variables impacting these differences, and many of them have to do with the passage of time. With Agile strategies in place, agencies and contractors are well-positioned to adapt to the specific needs of the acquisition –saving time and resources for both Government and Industry.

To succeed in Agile Government Contracting, leaders in both the Contracting and Program Management communities will need to build strong partnerships and jointly implement Agile methods. "Success" here is defined as reducing the resources (time and money) necessary for the Government to procure goods and services. Using the resources we have to procure the best products and services at the best price is a more reasonable (and effective) goal than simply throwing more resources at the problem. Many times, more resources just lead to more complexity. Guidelines for how to do so within the regulations will be detailed later in this book.

This book demonstrates how Agile delivers positive results by using a discovery process of ***iterative incremental development*** methods, based on Lean Manufacturing principles.

According to the report *Effective Practices and Federal Challenges in Applying Agile Methods, GAO-12-681, July 27, 2012, Appendix IV: Federal Projects,* examples of successfully applying Agile practices in the Government arena already include:

Global Combat Support System-Joint Increment 7
Agency: Department of Defense, Defense Information Systems Agency
System description: Supports logistics operations such as mission supplies for military personnel.
Agile approach: Scrum
Estimated cost: $192.3 million over a 5-year period

Enterprise Applications Competency Center Materials Management Initiative
Agency: National Aeronautics and Space Administration
System description: Supports receipt, warehousing, inventory, and issuance of operating materials.

Agile approach: Scrum
Estimated cost: $6.6 million

Occupational Health Record-keeping System
Agency: Department of Veterans Affairs, Veterans Health Administration
System description: Supports private employee health records.
Agile approach: Scrum
Estimated cost: $20 million for development and operation

Patents End-to-End
Agency: Department of Commerce, Patent and Trademark Office
System description: Supports end-to-end electronic patent processing.
Agile approach: Scrum
Estimated cost: $150 million over 5 years

The title ***Agile*** *Government Contracting* begs the question, "What does *Agile* mean in this book?" A complete answer will be developed in a later chapter, but in summary, ***Agile means using any of the Lean principles that improve the probability of a successful procurement in an environment of high complexity and uncertainty.***

Agile uses the principles of Lean Manufacturing, developed and proven by the Toyota Production System, because it is now generally accepted wisdom that Lean can be applied to both tangible and intangible products and services to improve delivery time, reduce cost and improve quality simultaneously. While the procurement process does not *manufacture* items, it does respond very effectively to Lean principles. Buying goods and services, at its core, is the effective application of available resources to execute a *process.* This book shows how Lean principles make the *procurement process* more efficient and effective.

Agile ***Government*** *Contracting* begs a second question, "Why does it appear to focus only on the Department of Defense (DoD) and ignore other equally important departments?" Unfortunately, it was a matter of constraints. While the Department of Veterans Affairs is the largest, and the Department of Health and Human

Services' Acquisition Regulation (HHSAR) and the Department of Homeland Security Acquisition Manual (HSAM) both supplement the Federal Acquisition Regulation (FAR), all certainly deserve similar treatment, to name only three examples. This book simply had to limit its scope as a matter of expediency.

That being said, we do look forward to producing a second edition with expanded coverage in those and other areas. In the meantime, we ask for your good grace in recognizing and using the obvious parallels and overlaps to your advantage. And should you be so inclined, we would welcome your contributions of any agency-specific content or challenges for the next edition. Simply email them to John Stenbeck at jstenbeck@gr8pm.com or Kevin Jans at kevin@skywayacquisition.com.

A clarifying note on CO vs. KO: Throughout this book we use the acronym CO to refer to a "contracting officer". In certain parts of the Department of Defense, the term "CO" refers to "Commanding Officer". Therefore, those agencies (such as the US Army and US Special Operations Command) use the acronym "KO" to refer to the contracting officer. We chose to use the acronym "CO" since it is more prevalent, and honestly, because it is easier recognize.

The subtitle of this book also begs a question by stating this book is applicable to Prime and Sub-Contractors. Yet, one could accuse our content of showing a decided "bias" towards the Government. How can that be? Why is that so?

The reason for citing so many Federal regulations is to help the Government personnel who control any decision "go Agile." For the ***leaders*** of the various Departments, Commands, and Agencies, this book provides a vision of how Agile can be accomplished and a look at validated models for guiding and controlling its implementation. For the ***Contracting Officers*** and ***Program Managers,*** it explains, using highly detailed, specific regulations, and practical examples, how they can ***legally participate*** in the ***information sharing*** that is critical in order to facilitate Agile approaches that will leverage Contractors' expertise to deliver better, faster, and more cost-effective solutions for our Government. The citations are the bridge we've built because it saves a huge amount of time and negotiating for all parties!

Without clear direction from the regulations, no responsible Government representative will act in a way that risks violating the strict legal standards they must follow, or that cannot be defended using the regulations. Doing so would mean unwisely risking their job or possibly facing civil or criminal legal action.

This book serves the Government contracting community by giving them the intense, deep research needed to intelligently discuss the regulations that open up procurements using Agile approaches. It also gives actual case studies (with some facts changed to align with Procurement Integrity Act requirements) that show this ***can*** be done. While Agile is not the norm in Government contracting, sending multi-million dollar proposals to a CO over EMAIL was not the norm in the past, yet today, 25% or more of proposals are digital only. That one change (which not all agencies have embraced yet) is an example of Agile thinking. It saves a great deal of time and money up front as well as storage and disposal time later. Processes that seemed unusual and even counter-productive just a few years ago are now becoming common- place – or soon will be.

An example of the impact of incremental change toward Agile: In 2002, Kevin had to decide what to do with boxes of old proposals that had been stored in a conference room now needed for another purpose. Those documents were 5 years old and the contract had been completed, but the files were still sensitive under the Procurement Integrity Act. Rather than just move them to another conference room and ignore them, Kevin shredded the 10 copies and kept only the originals in a locked safe. This cut the 'footprint' of this ONE proposal by 90%. Insane, yes. Common? Yes (especially without digital-only proposal submittals). Thus, not requiring paper copies has already moved Government contracting one small step in the right direction. Let's keep going!

A. What Department, Command and Agency Leaders Must Do

Over the last decade, it has become obvious to organizations of all types that the key driver of success is ***customer delight,*** which translates to ***constituent satisfaction.*** This means that ***winning the budget battles*** in Washington, D.C. (or anywhere else in America) is remarkably similar to winning the battle for consumer dollars worldwide.

First, Command and Agency leaders must ***understand the changing reality*** where they find themselves operating.

Over the last decade, everywhere on the globe – inside American Government and outside too – the rate of ***disruptive innovation*** in information technology has declined from majestic heights to merely exceptional levels. However, advances in innovation in other fields – like bioengineering, nanoscale science, and combinatorial chemistry – have expanded to fill that vacuum, and even accelerated the growth curve!

At the same time, the rate of ***incremental innovation*** has increased because smart phones, XML coding on the Internet, and social media sites are enabling innovation at speeds difficult to comprehend. These technologies allow information to proliferate and be leveraged from new selling venues like EZ RFP, to smart phone applications that notify offerors of Government RFP changes in real time. The expanding access to ever-more information has increased the sense of uncertainty and the desire for simplification for both Government and industry participants. (See the discussion on Disruptive and Incremental Innovation later in this book.)

Along the way, technology has ***fundamentally altered*** the process of innovation so it permanently advances on a non-linear growth curve. This technology-driven process improvement has created a ***vertical down-shift in the cost*** of finding the best possible solution because it reduces the cost of iterating by many ***rough orders of magnitude (ROM).***

That technology-driven process improvement means *the cost of exploration and experimentation* has been so *dramatically re-*

duced that discovering solutions that are *both* more effective and less costly is now completely possible.

This new dynamic can be seen in the advances driven by Lean principles and Agile development in industries as varied as automotive, commercial and rail transportation vehicles, as well as integrated circuits, pharmaceuticals, and software. Those same Lean principles will dynamically change the features, functionality, and cost of everything from fighter jets, tanks and aircraft carriers to micro-UAVs, battlefield medicine, and personnel management systems.

There is no reason that Government procurements should cost more and take longer simply because there are more of them. Just like production and technology innovations, the results should get better and cost less. The Traditional strategies of the past tie the CO and Program Managers to models that are now slower and more costly. (Consider how much you paid for your first flat screen TV versus how much are they now!)

Innovations and Agile thinking can create the same effect for COs and Program Managers. Digital-only proposals are a radically simple and clearly effective example of this technology driven shift.

Leveraging this new ***technology-driven process improvement,*** however, has proven tricky. Nowhere has it been trickier than in Agile Government Contracting and Agile Project Management (APM). Moving Government acquisitions from traditional ***prescriptive processes,*** with detailed specifications, to ***discovery processes***, with iterative and adaptive methods means organizations and people must change.

Department, Command and Agency Leaders, as well as Contracting Officers and Program Managers must now facilitate ***discovery processes*** rather than ***prescriptive ones.*** They must embrace exploration and experimentation and *balance it with control* through iterative and adaptive techniques. Many of the tools and processes to improve acquisitions are already available through these key regulations:

- **Federal Acquisition Regulation (FAR)**
- **Federal Acquisition Streamlining Act of 1994 (FASA) (Pub. L. 103-355)**

- **Federal Acquisition Reform Act (FARA) of 1995 (Pub. L. No. 104-106, 110 Stat. 186 and,**
- **Clinger-Cohen Act of 1996 (Pub. L. No 104–106).**

These reforms have been in place for nearly 10 years. The principles of Agile are already embedded in the regulations. The CO and Program Manager need only embrace a perspective of "discovery" to take advantage of these solutions.

This means organizations need to embrace, leverage and capitalize on the contracting approaches, management procedures, and progress metrics they already have in the FAR for guiding and measuring the discovery process in order to leverage the new lower-cost, higher-value performance their customers and constituents expect and demand.

Since there are already Parts of the FAR that allow for Agile techniques, **we do not need a new "Agile" Part of the FAR.**

Contracting officers simply need to be empowered to use the authority and responsibility of ***FAR 1.602*** to execute using the combination of Agile tools that already exist. Agile is about cutting away things that are not needed and defined in Lean as avoidable or unavoidable waste. Agile is not about adding new processes and more steps to "streamline" the process. Experience shows these additional "improvements" nearly always cost more and do less.

The acquisition plan should integrate the need of the Government user and the capability of the contractor. Between these two needs, lies a uniquely designed acquisition plan that the current regulations allow. Agile is about a quest to simplify the complex. What if a CO asked what he/she could take OUT of a source selection plan instead of adding more?

> "With any great design, the best result is revealed not when there is nothing left to add, but when there is nothing left to *take away*. (Antoine de Saint-Exupéry).

It is not a surprise that the transformation to Agile Government Contracting is proving difficult! Difficult or not, the ***Clinger-Cohen***

Act mandates COs and PMs ***consider*** these Agile approaches. Agile strategies may not apply in every case, but certainly must be considered in every case. What if COs and PMs approached each acquisition with this mindset of uniqueness, of Agile flexibility, and incremental innovation? How much more efficient could the process be? How many more targeted, applicable and effective proposals would offerors submit? How much faster could COs and PMs supply the valuable goods and services needed by the DOD? How much less would this whole process cost?

The Agile concepts explained in this book show that smaller, incremental acquisitions are easier to manage and have a higher probability of delivering useful, workable solutions than comprehensive procurements. It also describes approaches where delivery, implementation, and testing of workable systems or solutions occur in discrete increments.

However, many agencies continue to increase the size, complexity and broad-reach of Government contracts through multiple-award Indefinite-Delivery Indefinite-Quantity (IDIQ) contracts. There are various arguments for using these IDIQ contracts. One is the economies of scale (such as the USAF Commodities Council and Strategic Sourcing Initiatives). Another is the argument that the larger the contract, the easier it is to award a "one-and-done" strategy every five years instead of awarding small contracts every few years.

However, these cumbersome, bloated contracts are not delivering the efficiencies promised. Some of them actually cost more per unit. Most of them cost more per transaction, and nearly all of them place yet another person or process between the user and the supplier – all in the name of "efficiency". That efficiency may work for widgets and highly commoditized products like paper clips, computer screens, and tires. However, for many COs and PMs, the importance of unique requirements gets drowned in a quest to homogenize all requirements.

In the end, the customer is again paying more and getting less.

CO NOTE: The most successful source selections Kevin managed were when he awarded smaller contracts for a variety of services instead of trying to push them all together. For example, while as Special Operations Command (SOCOM), he bought ATVs, vehicle testing services, armored vehicles, and vehicle communications systems. Because of their overlapping requirements, Kevin could have merged these all into a giant, complex "SOCOM Vehicle Enhancement Contract (or some such similar name). However, the PM was more concerned about getting the best solution for each part of these customers and was not blinded by the "efficiency" of one integrated solution. As a result, rather than running one large source selection for a disparate series of goods and services that were loosely tied together by the overall SOCOM vehicle program, they focused on running five different acquisitions using a variety of solutions (including 3 source selections, a sole source award, and a limited competition) over a 12 month period that involved 16 companies and executed over $100M in contracts.

Compare that to how long it takes to develop one large SOW that overlaps these "vehicle related" program, develop a broad acquisition strategy, write the Draft RFP, address and combine the concerns of a diverse group of vendors (who would likely have to build teams to do every part of the work), then compete and award one large contract for over $100M for such a diverse amount of goods and services.

HINT: it's ***A LOT longer than 12 months*** in every contracting office Kevin has worked. A $100M program can take a full year just to get the requirement solidified and a draft RFP released. It could be two years or more to award the contract. All the while, the customer (and the taxpayer) and waiting for their contractual support.

Beyond that legislative mandate and the playing field where human communities compete requires innovation and agility to create or maintain any competitive or economic advantage, military or civilian.

Therefore, Department, Command and Agency leaders must ***embrace the responsibility*** of driving, guiding, and managing the organizational change that must occur to align their teams with the ***changing reality*** where they find themselves operating.

Second, Department, Command and Agency leaders must also ***champion*** the generally accepted wisdom that ***Lean principles***, the intellectual source of Agile practices, can be applied to Government acquisitions of both tangible and intangible products and services. Doing so simultaneously leads to improved delivery times, reduced costs, and improved quality.

While the claim of "better, faster, cheaper" may seem improbable or impossible, Lean delivers these results using several basic, quantifiable principles harnessed for procurements in both commercial and Government arenas.

Because there are enormous differences between developing tangible and intangible products, as well as between large capital and speed-to-capability projects, the process of analyzing needs and defining features varies widely.

As Figure 1.2 shows, what the various Agile approaches share is a beginning stage characterized by defining requirements and setting boundaries; an intermediate stage characterized by solution development; and a final stage characterized by scaling to production-level quantities.

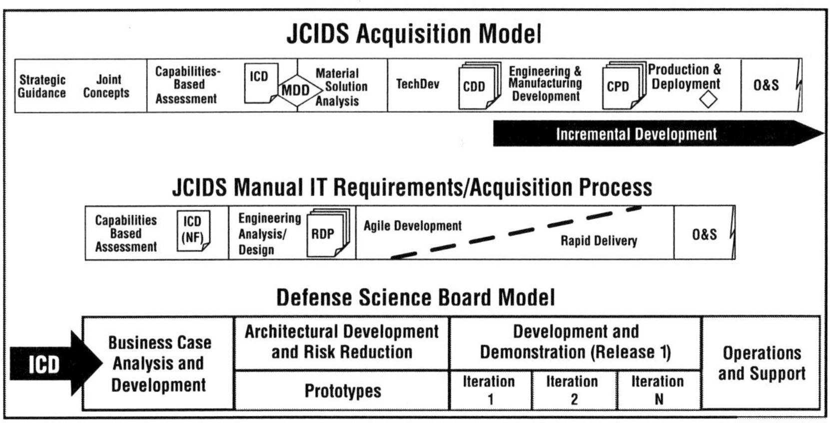

Figure 1.2 – Comparison of Basic Acquisition Models

Billions of dollars in contracted services each year are not subject to DoD requirements or documents and could benefit from Agile practices. Therefore, it is worth noting that Agile contracting may be applied to one part of the procurement process ***even if it is not used for the entire acquisition.*** Examples include the huge amount of Government contracting that never interfaces with the Joint Capabilities Integration and Development System (JCIDS) or the Defense Science Board Acquisition Process for I.T. Models shown (such as the Department of Health and Human Services (HHS) Enterprise Performance Life Cycle (EPLC) and the Center for Disease Control (CDC) implementation of the EPLC).

Figure 1.3 shows, at a high-level, a generic acquisition model for ***tangible*** products, such as waterfront construction. At the front end of the model, the Government documents a business case and does the necessary ***analysis*** to define the requirements. It then engages the services of a firm with the expertise to manage the construction process.

> **AGC NOTE:** To see what this analysis looks like, be on the lookout for the discussions on "acquisition strategy" throughout this book. This refers to, among other elements, the market research described in FAR Part 10. This is a grossly ignored part of the FAR. PMs and COs need to use the flexibility of FAR Part 10 to "market" their requirements to industry and get input on what is actually available in the market rather than solely focusing on what they 'want'. However, market research, itself, is a topic for the next book.

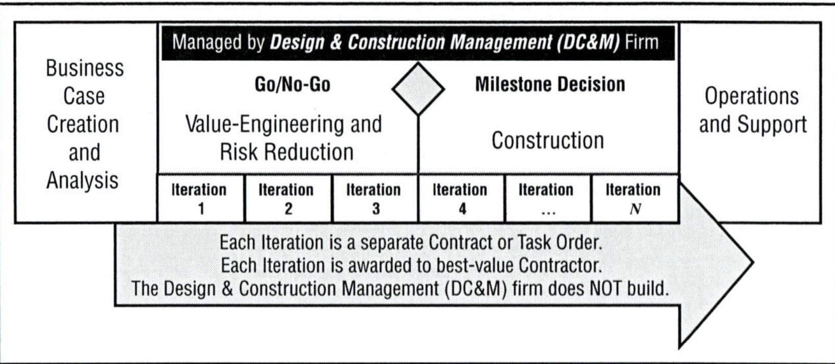

Figure 1.3 – Generic Acquisition Model for Tangible Deliverables

The Design & Construction Management (DC&M) firm does ***not*** perform the construction and may not even be responsible for performing the risk engineering. The DC&M firm is responsible for delivering on the Agile promise of faster, better, cheaper outcomes.

By having the DC&M firm manage the process, the Government extracts itself from the cat-and-mouse game of "winning" price reductions. Rather than Contractors inflating their prices by 30% so the Government procurement team can document a 15% price-reduction "win", the process becomes honest and transparent. Instead of awarding the contract to the $10 million low-bidder and ending up paying $22 million after years of delays and lawsuits, the Government gets the right outcome from the best-value Contractor, on time, for $16 million (i.e., the real price!).

How to do this, specifically and within the regulations, will be detailed later in this book.

Figure 1.4 shows a high-level, generic acquisition model for ***intangible*** products or services, such as software development. At the front end of the model, the Government documents a business case and does the analysis needed to define the requirements. It then engages the services of a firm with the expertise to manage the development process.

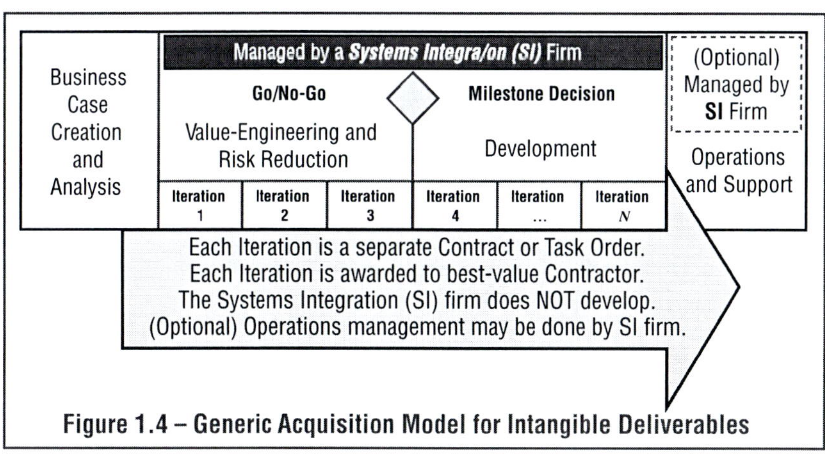

Figure 1.4 – Generic Acquisition Model for Intangible Deliverables

The Systems Integration (SI) firm does ***not*** perform the development and may not even be responsible for performing the system architecture and engineering.

Similar to the DC&M firm, the SI firm is responsible for delivering on the Agile promise of faster, better, cheaper outcomes, extracting the Government from the cat-and-mouse game of "winning" price reductions.

Again, how to do this, specifically and within the regulations, will be detailed later in this book.

Both models share the wisdom of using independent experts – whether they are called a Design & Construction Management (DC&M) firm or a Systems Integration (SI) firm – to counter the old Contractor adage, "Bid it low...and watch it grow!"

Lastly, Department, Command and Agency leaders must ***campaign for change*** that moves organizational culture from *"information **hoarding"*** to the critically necessary *"information **sharing"*** mindset.

To understand this leadership requirement, please consider SAP AG, the world leader in enterprise software and software-related services, headquartered in Walldorf, Germany. While SAP is not a Government, they have over $16 billion in annual revenue, more than 65,000 employees, and almost 250,000 customers in over 180 countries, so they likely deal with complexity on a level equivalent to most Departments, Commands, and Agencies.

In order for SAP's Enterprise Resource Planning (ERP) software solution to stay competitive, SAP had to move its vast ranks of employees, and a host of independent Value-Added Resellers (VARs), from an organizational culture of "information hoarding" to the "information sharing" mindset.

They accomplished this by creating a high profile place where Users could post questions and problems and the community could provide answers and solutions for all to see on their customer only website. They also defined three things that were critical. First, only the first 5 answer-solutions would be shared, incentivizing being quick to help. Second, they allowed the community to rate the value of those first 5 replies, which motivated providing quality help. And third, they offered "frequent flyer" type credits that could be used in the SAP store to acquire valuable merchandise, providing an immediate reinforcement of the sharing behavior.

Because the customer-only website was a key place to establish credibility as an expert, for both employees and VARs, and because speed and value were incentivized, there was an unmistakable shift to information sharing. Those who shared quickly and well were not only rewarded by SAP, the community also recognized them as real experts. Those who hoarded information simply ended up marginalizing themselves.

For Agile Government Contracting to work, Department, Command and Agency leaders need to be creative in developing, among other things, incentives for COs and Program Managers to apply the new approaches then share their questions, problems, and solutions in community forums providing personal safety and promoting risk taking, not punishing it.

Thus, Department, Command and Agency leaders must drive changes moving the organizational culture into an "information sharing" mindset by finding, funding, and supporting community forums and other similar initiates.

B. The Inconvenient, Inescapable Truth!

An ***inconvenient, inescapable truth*** is that the regulations are such a ***complex matrix of interlinking caveats***, they leave both Government personnel and Contractors often unable to tell which federal regulations govern them or precisely where they will ***"cross the line"*** and face stiff penalties or possibly criminal prosecution.

One glaringly challenging part of Agile Government Contracting hovers near that invisible line of transparency and communication between the Government and Contractors. Due to the strict rules governing the *"silent period"* (after RFP release and before the proposal due date) during solicitations, for many Contractors, the Government is underwhelming about communicating. Once the draft RFP or a BAA is issued, a Bidders Conference may be conducted to publicly discuss programmatic and performance issues. After the Bidders Conference, questions can be submitted to the Procurement Agency and an answer to each question is published to all registered Bidders via public correspondence. The "silent period" is only after the formal RFP release. Even then it is not technically "silent" – it is only that the CO is the only one who can do the "talking".

By waiting until the RFP has dropped to ask questions, offerors are working ***against*** both their own and the Government's best interest because it runs counter to the Contractor's best interest to ask critically important questions when the answers will be published for all their competitors to see. So the common wisdom, among Contractors, is that by the time transparent communication is available, contracts have already been won or lost. The best way for both industry and Government to address this problem is through market research on the Government side (see FAR Part 10) and targeting agencies and specific opportunities that are a "good fit" from the industry side.

> **"AGC NOTES":** For Agile Government contracting to produce real value this conundrum must be solved. If the Generic Acquisition Model shown in Figure 1.2 is used, for example, contracts for early Iterations can be used to clarify critically important questions in a way that keeps competition for the later, probably larger Iterations at the highest level. When contracted this way the early Iterations serve the Government's best interest by leveraging the high-discovery period.

Again, the reason this book cites so many Federal regulations is to help Contractors work with Contracting Officers or Program Managers by sharing the regulations that open up procurements allowing the Contractor to participate using an Agile approach. The citations are an investment we've made in order to save you a huge amount of time searching for them yourself.

A second ***inconvenient, inescapable truth***, from the Contractors' point of view, is however valuable Agile may be, unfortunately, the way contracts are awarded is ***overwhelmingly pricing focused.*** So even if a solution is clearly superior, if pricing is more than 10% or 15% above a technically acceptable competitor, the low-price Contractor will win the award. This sense of things has become more amplified as budget battles have shrunk the pool of available dollars.

Regardless of whether contractors agree with it, the truth is that price will always be a driving factor, just like it is in the commercial market. It may not be the *only* factor, but it is going to be a factor. Offerors ignore this fact at their peril. This book provides some Agile options to make the best use of price, even when it is not the driving factor.

> **CO HINT:** Price is rarely is the ONLY factor considered in a source selection, it is just the easiest to measure – especially after offerors have equalized their technical and past performance abilities.

That's why this book cites so many Federal regulations showing Agile options. In the end, it is still a Government decision to use Agile procurements, but this book serves Contractors by giving them easy access to clear, legal approaches that make it safe for COs or Program Managers to use Agile. The citations are the path we've marked in order to speed your journey in mastering Agile methods.

C. Capturing the Simple Victory

In a later chapter we will show, convincingly, that the principles of Lean as applied to Agile pivot on one core principle – ***eliminate waste!***

Eliminating waste is a simple, but not easy, victory because it is counter-intuitive in the Government-contracting arena. In our experience it is not easy because it means dispelling three persistent myths in order to open a new mindset where Agile choices are possible. The first being that all Government contracts can be fixed-price with fixed-quantities and fixed terms and conditions. The second myth is that Agile means embracing change without constraints. The third myth is that Agile is an all-or-nothing approach. All three are false; let's prove it!

The old Contractor saying, "Bid it low and watch it grow!" belies the first myth. The myriad number of change orders being processed right this moment also belies it. And finally, the federal regulations bely it.

Many acquisitions are fixed price with a fixed scope. For example, a CO awards a contract for 50 commercial All Terrain Vehicles (ATV). Even if the CO modifies the contract, the contract "scope" (which is to buy 50 ATVs) does not change. An "out of scope" changes would be using the same contract to buy, say, light bulbs.

However, the contract deliverables can be changed ***within*** the scope of the contract to take advantage of Agile techniques. For example, the user needs have changed enough that the ATVs now need to be a different color. That is not an out of scope change, it's a priced modification. Rather than create an adversarial environment where the contractor is expected to absorb this change (since there may be a cost associated with it), the Agile strategy is to collaborate on what other adjustments can be made to offset this cost? Perhaps they can delivered a few days later, or shipped to a different location to offset the costs. These creative, solution-focused strategies that use information sharing allow acquisitions, and contracts, to be faster, cheaper and better.

FAR 43.201 instructs, generally, that Government contracts should contain a ***changes clause*** that permits the Contracting Officer to make unilateral changes, in designated areas, within the general scope of the contract.

Additionally, ***Financial Management Regulation (FMR), DoD 7000.14-R, Volume 3, Chapter 8,*** in pertinent part, makes the Contracting Officer responsible for determining scope of work changes and determining whether a change is within the scope of a contract. It even goes on to say that within certain limits, appropriations may be available to fund scope cost growth.

Ask yourself, "If Government contracts really are fixed-price, fixed-delivery and fixed-terms and conditions, then why is any of this regulatory detail needed?" The answer is, they are not! Contracts should be designed to be fluid and adjustable ***within scope*** to meet the needs of a market full of innovation. Innovation is happening fast. Contracting officers need to consider how they can structure their contracts to capitalize, not be hampered by a lack of access to, these innovations.

Figure 1.5 shows contract scope as a rectangle and contract language – that is deliverables, terms and conditions, and schedule – as a square within that rectangle. The specific contract language (the square) can move and change shape, as long as it does not breach the out limits of the scope (the rectangle). The scope of the contract is, in simple terms, what problem the contract was awarded to solve.

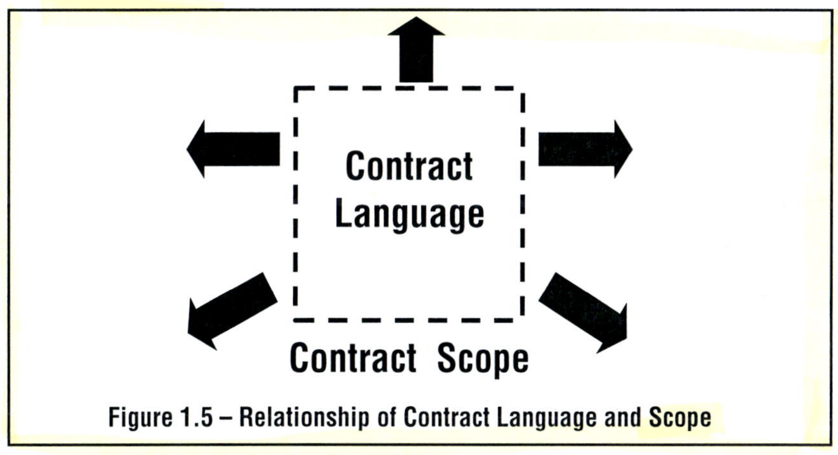

Figure 1.5 – Relationship of Contract Language and Scope

For example, the CO awards an IDIQ contract for $15,000,000 to buy up to 1,500 commercial ATVs. The contract solves the problem of the user needing ATVs. Over time, the Government may need to modify the contract to add different tires, upgrade the headlights, or use different brake pads,. These would all be modifications to the contract language (the square). However, this does ***not*** modify the contract "scope" (which is to buy 1,500 ATVs).

The second persistent myth, that Agile embraces change without limits, is proven false by one of Agile's own Best Practices. It is a best practice that both the scope of work – referred to as the Sprint or Iteration Backlog – and the duration of the Iteration are fixed. Beyond that, it is generally accepted that when Agile methods are being used in an arms-length transaction between two entities, the overall scope is defined by the boundaries of the contract even though the development and delivery of that scope may be flexible.

The third myth, that Agile is an all-or-nothing approach can be shown false by a quick review of any of the JCIDS, Defense Science Board, HHS – EPLC or CDC – EPLC Models. They all show Agile contracting as part of the procurement process even when it is ***not*** used for the entire acquisition.

Acceptance of these myths has led to the all-too-common RFP dictating specific, non-essential processes or steps, in an effort to be thorough enough, thereby forcing Contractors to change their processes in ways that increase complexity and drive up cost to the Government, simply to comply with the RFP.

So the first simple breakthrough is to reject those myths and acquire an open mind that recognizes Agile complies with contract boundaries, that COs have wide latitude to meet the contract's intent using in-scope contract changes, and that Program Managers can use Agile as a part of the acquisition process. Recognizing that the "new" reality already exists opens up possibilities where COs working with Program and Project Managers plan for changes – and maybe even use "scope swaps" to manage them – so that the Government receives the best possible value and the Contractor enjoys a mutually beneficial relationship in providing that value.

> **CO NOTE:** The term "scope swap" is not quite accurate since, as we have shown, out of scope changes breach the confines of the contract. However, these Agile strategies of neutral change modification or "requirement swaps" can be used within scope with much success when applied to in scope changes.

This Field Guide is intended to enable that bright new horizon!

D. Understanding this Field Guide

What Field Guide Means

This book serves as a ***field guide*** for Department, Command and Agency Leaders, Contracting Officers, Procurement Professionals, Program Managers, and Prime Contractors and Sub-Contractors by helping both Government and industry find a common path forward in this fast-paced environment. It will:

- Identify options that meet statutory and regulatory mandates.

- Provide specific step-by-step procedural outlines.
- Protect and support customers' needs within the statutory and regulatory requirements.

For most procurements, the Government has an immense range of contract-type options, yet it most often seems to choose Firm Fixed Price (FFP) or Cost Plus Fixed Fee (CPFF). While those options cover a range of possibilities, they are often inadequate for procurements where high uncertainty or high complexity exists.

Congressional mandates and Executive Branch demands for Government acquisitions to become more Agile are an acknowledgement of the challenges and highly publicized failures of using FFP or CPFF contracts when high uncertainty exists. CPFF seems to be the ideal contract type when there is high uncertainty in a requirement (because the fee is fixed regardless of what happens). However, the problem with poorly managed (and un-Agile) contracts on programs that fail is that the contractor gets a fixed-fee regardless of success. COs and PMs need to use Agile strategies to focus on program success, not just on who is left holding the risk of failure.

Yet, since moving forward is mandatory for both Government personnel and Contractors, the questions are, "What can be done?" and " How can progress be accomplished legally?"

This guide is intended to shine a light on new options that are characterized as Agile and point to the specific regulations authorizing their use.

What Field Guide Does Not Mean

First and foremost, this field guide is not a magic wand. It does not magically erase the unavoidable competitive acquisition process (as directed by the Competition in Contracting Act of 1984), the pressures faced by the Government to award contracts more quickly and efficiently, or the associated cost competition and time compression faced by contractors. Nor does it erase the rigorous work required of COs and Program Managers during every stage of an acquisition.

As the title implies, this guide covers Agile Government Contracting in general, but may feel, at times, largely focused on software development programs. That is because Agile acquisitions in Government – and the commercial world as well – have a longer track record of success in software, and a shorter, more recent one in tangible products and services.

Therefore, this book remains a field guide with coverage that has been researched, engineered, and designed to be *instructive, not exhaustive.* Thus, it avoids theoretical debates that, although interesting and well merited, lack the focus on practical, useful, concrete processes for moving forward, *if, when* and *where* Agile makes sense.

This field guide is carefully crafted to illuminate Agile specific topics and challenges in a way that can be read in a short time. If a detailed understanding is desired, the references to various FARs, DFARS, OMB Circulars, and Executive Orders can be consulted. Alternately, time can be spent investigating the details and case law guidance using the ***LexisNexis' Federal Contract Management*** reference or the ***Federal Acquisition Regulation site (farsite.hill.af.mil).***

Another great resource you may also wish to review is Kevin's blog at **www.skywayacquisition.com/blog.** It contains more case studies, examples and insights on this complex market.

CHAPTER

2

Core Agile Concepts

This chapter is not intended to be as much of a Field Guide as the rest of the book. Instead, the purpose is to provide an introduction to the core concepts of Agile so that readers can effectively use them in Agile procurements.

Agile Value Proposition ... in a Nutshell!

As strange as it sounds, companies, organizations, and communities, as well as Departments, Commands, and Agencies, do not actually want agility – or at least not agility for agility's sake. They want innovation! Organizations of all types have come to recognize over the last decade or so, that the economic drivers of success have moved from information to innovation.

> The economic drivers of success have moved from information to innovation.

As stated in our introduction, although the rate of information technology innovation has declined from majestic to "only" exceptional over the last decade, innovation in bioengineering, nanoscale science, combinatorial chemistry and sophisticated computer simulations filled any vacuum and accelerated the growth curve. Technology has fundamentally altered the innovation process to permanently advance on a non-linear growth curve. This technology-driven process change can be defined as a vertical shift that reduced, by rough orders of magnitude, the cost of iterating through uncertainty to find the best possible solution.

That technology-driven process change means the cost of exploration and experimentation has been so dramatically reduced that discovering solutions *both* more effective and less costly is now possible. This new dynamic can be seen in the advances driven by Lean manufacturing and Agile development in industries as varied as integrated circuits, pharmaceuticals, software, and automotive, commercial and rail transportation vehicles, and even support services.

Organizations and people must change when moving from the Traditional prescriptive processes, with detailed specifications, to discovery processes with experimental and exploratory methods. COs and Program Managers must now facilitate the discovery process rather than design detailed, prescriptive plans.

Executing projects using the correct Project Management framework ensures those projects maximize the positive impact of the assets and people deployed to deliver them. To accomplish this, professional Project Managers are increasingly being tasked by their organizations to synthesize the best practices of Traditional and Agile frameworks into an approach tailored to the environmental demands they face. Without a solid base of Agile Project Management knowledge, it is impossible for a Project Manager to effectively fulfill that responsibility.

Figure 2.1 shows what is strongly suggested by experience everywhere; the future of Project Management is hybrid projects.

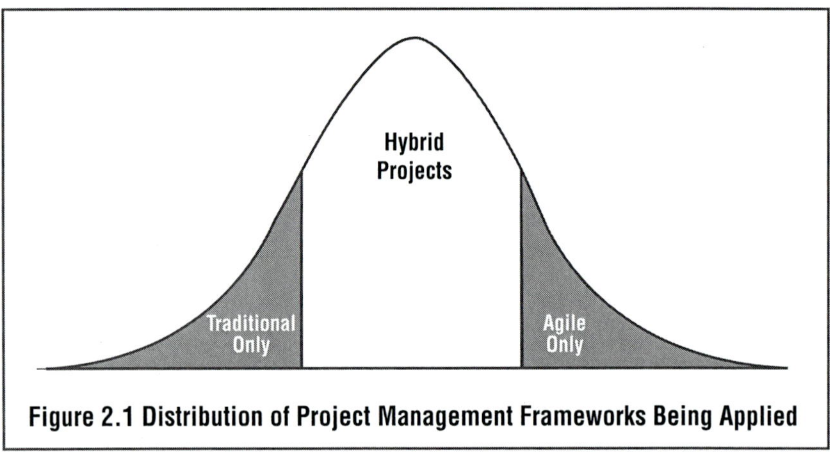

Figure 2.1 Distribution of Project Management Frameworks Being Applied

Hybrid projects are managed with a combination of Traditional and Agile practices or a combination of practices from multiple Agile frameworks.

Tomorrow's professional Project Manager cannot be effective without the ability to run hybrid projects using both Traditional and Agile frameworks!

A. What You Can't Not Know

The economic and competitive landscape is driven by innovation because innovation is so closely correlated with thriving and growing. The absence of innovation is correlated with failing and dying. However, to avoid confusion, a critical distinction needs to be made. Most often when someone says innovation, the hearer envisions what we designate as disruptive innovation.

Disruptive innovations *displace* an existing technology or business process in an unexpected way, creating new market value for a different or existing customer segment in a new or different way.

Small companies use disruptive innovation to level the playing field when competing against larger organizations. Disruptive innovation is the kind that makes the news and is featured in history books with names like Edison, Bell, Wright, more recently Jobs and Zuckerberg. Disruptive change fundamentally changes the way we do business in an industry or in life in general. The most obvious and recent example is the smart phone. The smart phone did not exist 15 years ago. Now, for 60% of Americans, their smart phone is the last thing they touch before the go to sleep and the first thing they touch when they wake up. If that's you, you know what disruptive innovation looks like.

While not on the level of the smart phone, examples of disruptive innovation in the Federal market include fundamental policy changes, as well as capitalizing on technology platforms to transform how the Government buys.

Federal Market is an example of a disruptive ***policy*** innovation you may well be familiar with already.

FAR 13.5 Test Program is another example of a policy innovation allowing COs to use Simplified Acquisition Procedures (SAP) to purchase commercial items and services for up to $6.5M. Since the current SAP threshold is $150,000, this policy change (a 40x increase in the size of the contract that a CO can compete and award) is literally and figuratively huge! Using a simple process, these acquisitions can be executed in under three weeks with adequate planning. Compare that with most $6M source selections often taking three months and it is a truly good disruptive innovation.

Agile Government Contracting (AGC) is not about spending more money more quickly. It is about using common sense business practices to buy products and services using speed, efficiency ***and*** competition. As we discuss in the SAP chapter, this Test Program expires on Jan 1, 2015. However, history predicts that it will be renewed – especially if books like this one show how it can enable Agile Government Contracting and produce great results!

Another example of a disruptive innovation is the ***FARSite*** online (http://farsite.hill.af.mil) ***technology platform.***

When Kevin first started using the online version of the Federal Acquisition Regulation (FAR) in 1999 at Wright Patterson AFB, he soon realized it was electronically searchable, someone else was updating it for free, and he got on board. It eventually evolved into the standard site for all FAR regulations. Another benefit was that unlike the printed versions the online version was updated in near real-time. Having a current version of the FAR at his fingertips that was searchable and accessible from anywhere was a game-changing event for him as a CO. ***Suddenly, being a CO was less about memorization and more about application.*** No more need to memorize the regulations because he could search the FAR site and within seconds have the answer. It was a really big deal!

Other examples of disruptive technology innovations in the federal market include www.FedBizOpps.gov, www.RFPEZ.SBA.gov and www.FedBid.com.

> **CO NOTE:** Kevin predicts that in the next few years, a new generation of COs will use tools like LinkedIn, Twitter, and Facebook to drive interest in Government RFPs. Sound crazy? So did being able to access a Facebook account from a desk at Special Operations Command. However, that happened in the Spring of 2012 when the impact of not using these social media tools finally outweighed the risks associated with accessing them from a Government computer.

As important as disruptive innovation is, it has a much smaller impact than the type of innovation we designate as incremental innovation. ***Incremental innovations*** *evolve* an existing technology or business process to create more market value for existing and new customer segments.

Big companies use incremental innovation to extend, expand, and renew the financial returns of their products and services within and between markets. Incremental innovation for products has created millions of dollars of sales in new niches. Incremental innovations, like Apple's iPad, have often enjoyed success because they were linked to a disruptive innovation, like Apple's App Store business model. Similarly, Amazon took their disruptive innovation – an online bookstore – and incrementally created the global marketplace now available. Likewise, Government contracting has used incremental innovation to improve the processes they already have.

Incremental Technology Innovations

Since 1999, FARSite has expanded to include nearly every federal department and agency's FAR Supplement, a clear example of incremental innovation following a disruptive one. Figure 2.2 shows the homepage banner of the FARSite so you can see all the participating groups. Each of the Agency icons is a link to that agency's FAR Supplement. What started as simply a FAR site, is now the home for all agencies' FAR supplements. It also includes free tools like ***FARSearch and Clause Logic.*** (Note: for a free demo of these tools, visit www.skywayacquisition.com.)

Another incremental technology innovation is the development of Wide Area Work Flow (WAWF) to expedite payments to Government contractors. WAWF created an automated invoicing and payment system. Despite being imperfect, WAWF, on a massive scale, has shaved days, weeks, or even months off the time it takes to pay contractors. The efficiency is especially important for small businesses because cash flow can mean the difference between keeping their doors open or not, directly impacts the COs ability to effectively compete contracts.

B. The Agile-Enterprise Model

Enterprise-level APM is being used in many industries including Aerospace and Defense, Automotive, Consumer and High Technology, Manufacturing, and Pharmaceuticals and Life Sciences. It is used to reduce costs, and improve product quality by shortening product lifecycles, reducing supply chain complexity, satisfying ever-increasing customer demands and even accelerating revenue.

Today, many organizations must deliver operational excellence across an extended enterprise. They must integrate outsourced providers and internal processes to create innovation based on decisions about their products throughout local, regional and global distribution networks. This enterprise model also applies to the Government. Agencies have ever-increasing footprints to manage as the world gets more and more global. For example, how many embassies does the State Department manage in nearly every country in the world? In how many states does the IRS have offices? How many countries does Special Operations Command need to be able to deploy, sustain and support its operators? These Government agencies are large, complex organizations. In general terms, the Government agencies that run well are run as flat, innovative, *Agile* enterprises. The ones that are bloated and inefficient are run with ***Traditional***, stove-pipe, top-down hierarchy.

Companies as diverse as Bayer, Flextronics, GE Medical Systems, Heinz, Johnson & Johnson, Lockheed Martin, McAfee, McDonald's, Philips, Qualcomm, Siemens, and Tyco Healthcare, are using Agile processes to drive positive business results.

Speed-to-market and ***time-to-volume*** determine ***time-to-value***, and success, in many challenging markets. Agile processes transform time into a competitive advantage by using strategies and tactics enabling teams to align with enterprise goals.

> The driving variable in today's environment is ***time-to-value*** and Agile processes transform ***time*** into a ***competitive advantage*** on every kind of battlefield!

Speed-to-market connotes the need to bring a product to market as quickly as possible to create or defend an advantage.

Time-to-volume describes how long it takes to develop a product from first prototype or Iteration until it can be delivered in production volumes.

Time-to-value expresses the time between the initial delivery of a product or service and when a defined business, agency or command goal, such as a quantifiable financial return or a qualitative, intangible metric such as lives protected, is achieved.

C. Scheduling Portfolios and Programs

To integrate multi-project architecture and engineering, the portfolio- and program-level planning processes must be expressed as a ***Roadmap***, which begins with defining the key features of the various products or services being offered or sought in the organization's development plan. Those defining key features are called the ***minimal marketable features (MMF)***, for each component or product, in the program or portfolio.

Minimal marketable features (MMF) are the smallest set of features providing the level of functionality required to fulfill customer expectations and create a competitive distinction.

To begin, the appropriate level of management creates a ***central feature list***, a rough sketch or superset of the critical functionality representing the MMF. It represents the vision for current product development as well as the potential of what could eventually be developed. Central feature lists are used as input for planning the Roadmap and Releases. It is not necessary to wait until all features are defined before starting development of the initial product functionality.

Roadmaps are a planning tool used to align Agile's short development cycles with a desired longer term result. Roadmaps include descriptions of proposed functionality and anticipated delivery timeframes, typically with fiscal-quarter granularity, for 9 to 36 months. Roadmaps have a one-to-many relationship with ***Releases*** and contain ***Feature Stories.***

Releases are a planning tool used to guide development cycles to the desired business result. Releases include ***User Stories*** and intended delivery timeframes, typically with Iteration-level granularity, for 3 to 12 months.

After the central feature list is created, each feature is documented as a ***Feature Story*** either by management, or more likely their designee(s), as part of the planning process.

Feature Stories document a business goal as specific pieces or components of business functionality with perceived value for the customer or user.

Feature Stories are the largest stories and are used to capture the description of important functionality at a high level for planning Roadmaps and Releases. They have a one-to-many relationship to User Stories and Tasks.

Employing Feature Stories for Scheduling

Feature Stories are documented by writing down the goal and specific piece or component of functionality the user needs in order to perceive value. The Feature must be expressed with enough granularity so the approximate effort of developing that Feature can be expressed at a ROM level. Defining, even roughly, the approximate effort of a Feature Story enables initial prioritizing and reduces the likelihood of radical, indiscriminate scope reductions later.

Experience has shown that estimates become less accurate as they forecast events that are farther out in the future and that estimates are asymmetrically distributed, with the probability of under-estimating exceeding the probability of over-estimating. Because Feature Stories are long-range forecasts, they can only be estimated at the ROM level, but are useless if they cannot be estimated.

Experience has also shown a Feature will, many times, appear necessary or valuable when first conceived, but often gets abandoned when replaced by a better, or simply different, alternative as the project progresses and additional customer discovery and learning occurs. Therefore, the team documents the details of a Feature Story when they decompose it into User Stories and not before. At that point in time, the probability of actual development is high enough to justify spending the resources on detailed planning and is referred to as the ***last responsible moment.***

Last responsible moment occurs when the advantage of acquiring additional, valuable information or insight is balanced by the potential downside of delaying the decision any further, as shown in Figure 2.3.

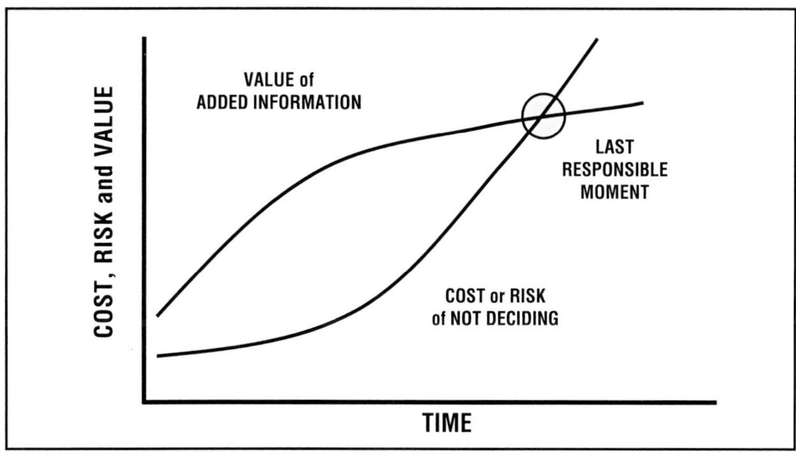

FIGURE 2.3 Concept of Last Responsible Moment

The concept of a last responsible moment is a guideline, not a scientific-formula type of concept, and assumes that, over time, decisions move from enjoying maximum benefit of delay to risking maximum cost of delay. Quantifying the benefits and costs in a highly accurate way is not needed because the evaluation is intended to be qualitative.

Feature Stories (and User Stories) are a deceptively simple way of integrating purpose-driven customer conversations with drawings, prototypes, and small segments of development to unlock the powerful human genius imbedded in experiencing tangible samples relating to the whole solution. Those kinds of conversations allow customers to evaluate small steps of progress and pro vide "actionable insight" about the optimal way for the project to be successful.

User Stories are the most common stories and include necessary, important details like acceptance criteria, tests, and a "definition of done". They are used for planning Iterations.

The power of this approach becomes a "blinding flash of the obvious" when you remember that written words are very tenuous expressions of the unavoidably complex content of most projects. Because, as the saying goes, "The greatest myth about communication is...that it has happened", vigilance is required to prevent misinterpretation. Frequent conversations between the customer, users, and the team create a tremendously powerful antidote to this common problem. Feature Stories prevent forgetting to discuss important functionality at the appropriate time and thus support robust estimating and planning.

To succeed, a project must take information from a variety of customers, users, business analysts, technical experts and the team, then understand and integrate it. While this occurs, the team is also trying to properly allocate resources and juggle quality tradeoffs, other current features, and partially described expected future features. When that environment is visualized, it becomes clear why it is impossible to perfectly predict the path of development for the best solution.

In such an unpredictable environment, the most logical approach is to make decisions based on the reliability of the information available.

In APM, decisions are made at the optimal point when two factors intersect; "the last responsible moment" and "the best available information." Decisions made at the last responsible moment are not made prematurely as important information may emerge. That information constitutes the best available information, in part, because it is as complete as possible. Making decisions before that point in time means the best available information is not yet available. Making them after implies inducing avoidable risks and problems.

Many things change – commonly, the customer's understanding of their need and the best solution – as successive Iterations produce new learning. That is why Agile uses Feature Stories for planning and requires User Stories for development. These two types of Stories facilitate decision making at the intersection of the last responsible moment and the best available information.

Stories are a multifaceted device with tangible and intangible aspects. They are composed of a ***written*** piece, the tangible "Card", representing customer requirements and used in the planning process; an intangible ***promise*** (or commitment) to have conversations with the customer, user or technical experts, as needed, to identify details of the Story at the appropriate granularity to enable planning and development of the solution, and a written, tangible ***collection*** of tests demonstrating when a story is complete. The key is that Stories describe customer value, as Feature Stories or User Stories, and facilitate planning and information management.

D. Relating Stories to the PMBOK® Guide

The ***PMBOK® Guide*** defines a specific taxonomy, or arbitrary logical device, called a Work Breakdown Structure (WBS) for organizing information with five levels. The highest level is Objective, followed in descending order by Phase, Work Package, Activity and Task. The higher levels have ideas expressed in broader, less specific information while the lower levels have the same ideas expressed in greater detail. The WBS is a very useful tool for the immense amount of information that must be collected and managed in any project.

APM, by contrast, uses a taxonomy called a Feature Breakdown Structure (FBS) for organizing information. However, because APM has not been codified into a standard, there are a number of naming conventions for the various levels. One of the most common identifies the highest level as Product, followed in descending order by Theme, Epic, Story and Task. Similarly to WBS, the higher levels have broader, less specific information while the lower levels have greater detail. The FBS is a very useful tool for the same reason as the WBS.

The WBS and FBS share several aspects. First, the naming conventions are figurative in the sense that they describe what they contain in general terms relative to the other levels. (There is not a precise definition of the difference between an Activity and a Task, or an Activity and a Work Package. Likewise there is not a precise differentiation between Story and Task or Story and Epic.) The higher-level term, in both schemes, is bigger while the lower-level term is smaller. The purpose of both the WBS and FBS is to facilitate managing project information, not to impose a rigid set of size criteria.

A common cause of confusion is the use of the term User Story to describe a Card. Based on the size of the *idea*, and the amount of detail present or absent, the Card can be either a Feature Story or a User Story. Cards can be classified as a Theme, Epic, Story or Task, yet it is not uncommon to refer to all of them as a "story". This confusion can be avoided by using more accurate terminology when expressing information or by asking clarifying questions when others are expressing information.

Likewise, a common cause of frustration, especially for those new to APM, is the fact that Stories do not document deep, specific detail like the specifications used in Traditional Project Management. Rather than writing all the details in the story, the development team and the customer have promised to have a conversation about the details at the point when they become important. The point of frustration occurs when neither the team nor the customer can point to the card months later and use it to avoid ownership of a problem by saying something like, "I wrote that disclaimer right here" or "I made that part of the spec right there". Many participants in projects have learned how to "use the details" for coverage when a problem comes storming along.

Lastly, as stated above, Stories include a written, tangible *collection* of tests. Those tests demonstrate, in measurable terms, the agreement between the customer and the team about a Story's completion and acceptance. This facet of User Stories meets the vital need to clearly understand the customer's expectations. By recording acceptance tests on the card, the User Story captures those expectations in a measurable form. For the team, the tests are written reminders about the Story expectations and help clarify when they are done.

The *PMBOK® Guide* describes a project as, "A temporary group activity designed to produce a unique product, service or result."

That definition presupposes decisions have been made about what unique problem the product, service or result will solve. It implies only what the solution will deliver.

Agile Project Management, by way of contrast, presupposes that an accurate and exact knowledge of the problem and its solution do not exist – actually cannot exist – in advance. Agile assumes that an inescapable part of the development process is discovery and learning. Discovery occurs as the project moves through the ***Cone of Uncertainty,*** encountering the unknown and the unexpected. Discovery is shared with the Customer, who is most qualified to decipher and interpret the meaning of the discoveries. Then, the customer and team translate the discoveries into learning, providing proper perspective on the impact on priorities. Using that learning, the team acts as a trusted advisor, presents options to the Customer, translates those options as potential Features, and negotiates when and how to implement those Features.

E. Understanding the Cone of Uncertainty

APM embraces the idea of a Cone of Uncertainty because complex problems cannot be fully defined in advance. APM uses a scientifically validated empirical process control approach – transparency, inspection, and adaptation – to focus the team on quickly delivering results that move through the Cone of Uncertainty towards a solution in the midst of emerging requirements.

Cone of Uncertainty describes how unknown facets of the problem decrease over time as discovery and learning occur. During solution development, the amount of uncertainty declines in a way that can often be correlated to variances in estimates. Plotting these variances over time creates a cone or funnel shape, as shown in figure 2.4.

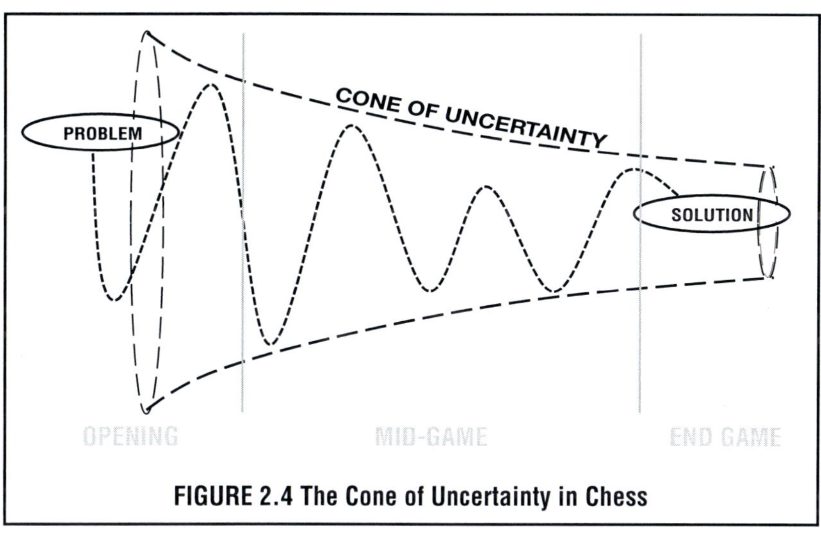

FIGURE 2.4 The Cone of Uncertainty in Chess

Moving from Agile as a micro-dynamic, team management framework and scaling it up to a macro-dynamic, organizational framework is a bit like moving from playing checkers to playing chess. Chess is clearly more complicated than checkers and offers more challenges and rewards.

In higher levels of chess competition, there are three general objectives during the Opening. The first objective is to achieve better positioning. The second objective is to create dynamic, competitive imbalances favoring your side and aligning with strategic Mid-Game choices. You may seek to improve your advantage or blunt the competitor's advantage. Finally, a third objective is to lure the opponent into positions where you have an advantage or feel more comfortable.

Similarly, the opening moves in APM are intended to move the project through the areas of least clarity and greatest flexibility by aligning the strategic vision of the organization with the highest probability of success.

The Mid-Game in chess follows the Opening and blends into the End Game. The three major objectives in the Mid-Game are king safety, force, and mobility. King safety can be compared to strategic alignment because a well-executed attack on the king can render other advantages irrelevant; much like the iPad rendered tablet PCs irrelevant. Force, often referred to as Material, is similar to market share or market position in the real world. If all other factors are equal, material advantage will favor the larger competitor because they have the resources to gain more material and create a decisive advantage. Before the dawn of the Internet and options like the Amazon marketplace, material advantage was much more insurmountable. The new electronic marketplace options have amplified mobility, expressed as creativity and flexibility in the real world, because the scope of actions and segments to specialize in has become virtually unlimited. Because mobility must be managed at the enterprise-level, the demand for Agile Project Leaders who can lead efforts to scale Agile to the enterprise has reached a fever pitch in the marketplace.

Interestingly, the chess game analogy can be overlaid on the S-curve familiar to Traditional Project Managers all over the world (see Figure 2.5) with many of the same conclusions. It also draws out another conclusion shared with the Cone of Uncertainty. The later a change is made in the solution development cycle, the more risky and expensive it is to implement.

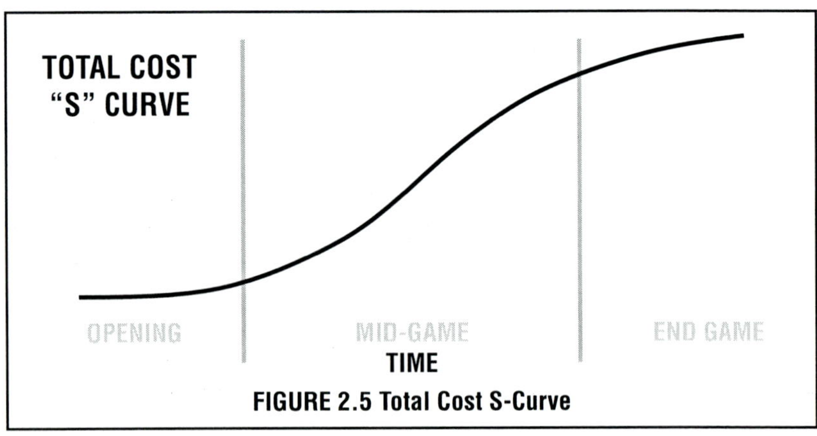

FIGURE 2.5 Total Cost S-Curve

Recognizing and leveraging a planning process that properly manages the discoveries and learning available in the early part of the cycle creates advantages later. The Iterative planning process embraced by APM is exactly that type of process. It begins with developing ROM estimates, or what APM refers to as ***Sizing***, for each of the Feature Stories. APM uses a tool called Affinity Estimating to do this quickly and cost effectively.

Affinity Estimating is a technique for estimating a large number of Stories in a quick, cost-effective way, which supports the planning and decision-making process. It is typically used to plan Roadmaps or Releases. Since Roadmaps are critical and high-level, they are usually done with a co-located team of executives.

F. Identifying Minimal Marketable Features (MMF)

For many projects and stakeholders, the primary objective is to create a competitive advantage, or distinction, by being first to market. Being a first mover creates the opportunity to capture massive market share, generate premium pricing margins, and possibly enjoy cost savings. In order to achieve the goal of being first to market, it is often necessary to tightly focus the project on quickly delivering the Minimal Marketable Feature set.

Identifying and refining the project focus down to the MMF provides an early and important opportunity to engage stakeholders in participatory decision-making. Moving from a broad central feature list to a Roadmap with the most important features being developed first is the process where the MMF is defined in an actionable way.

Once the MMF has been defined and sized, the velocity can be calculated to determine the probability of meeting any given release date. If the release date is not soon enough, the MMF must be reassessed to see what features could be modified or eliminated to achieve the desired market timetable. With each cycle of refinement and analysis, clarity about when any given set of features can be delivered becomes clearer.

When the team decides that the optimal plan has been acknowledged, the results should be documented in a ***business case.***

Business Cases are written documents explaining how the use of resources is aligned with the accomplishment of a goal or the implementation of a needed change.

A compelling business case leaves no doubt that benefits outweigh costs and risks. (Teaching exactly how to create one is outside of the scope of this book, but a quick outline is appropriate and included here.) The business case should include:

1. A compelling executive summary
2. The business environment and the context of the customer's needs
3. The various options considered for meeting those needs and the option chosen
4. Success metrics for the proposed solution
5. Analysis of the related cost/benefit and financial ratios

The goal is to identify the problem and impacted stakeholders, systems and business processes the project seeks to help, then demonstrate that the project clearly and directly solves it.

G. Creating Value-Driven Deliverables

Value-driven deliverables are the output of development effort contained in each time box. ***Time boxes*** are cycles of development focused on clarifying the product value stream creating customer value – from project charter to final deliverables – by integrating regular customer feedback. The value stream begins with the customer's vision, which proceeds through various stages of clarification and elaboration as development progresses.

Because value-driven deliverables may be the most recognized, differentiating, and critical success factor in APM, it is crucial for the team to understand them. The customer/proxy must convey to the team, early in the project, *what* is envisioned and must be delivered, *who* the key stakeholders are, and *how* the stakeholders will use the deliverables.

Identifying all the stakeholders and defining the MMF is part of an adaptive, value-driven planning process. All such planning approaches use the concepts of decomposition and progressive elaboration to identify the incremental pieces required to produce the desired solution.

It is interesting that many Agile aficionados are surprised to hear that the concepts of decomposition and progressive elaboration have existed in the *PMBOK® Guide* for many years. It is just as interesting that many Traditional Project Management aficionados are astonished to hear that APM has used these accepted concepts to refine the project delivery process in powerful and useful ways.

The planning process, starting with the central feature list and moving through the creation of feature stories and affinity estimates, produces a Roadmap and Release Plans. This is the first, and highest-level example of the Agile value-driven delivery process.

MAPP Day at Intel® is such a process, successfully institutionalized to create a continuous flow of innovative breakthroughs for multiple decades. ***MAPP*** stands for ***Make A Project (or Program) Plan*** and dedicated facilitators guide the process.

Intel® has demonstrated that establishing a value-driven delivery process, while neither quick nor painless, is well worth the investment. While it is not easy, it is amazingly effective when the right tools are employed, accompanied by adequate training and process standards.

The purpose of the value-driven delivery process is to help stakeholders clarify and articulate their values and priorities early in the Project Management process and create a mechanism where follow-up conversations define and direct the team's work efforts. Another purpose is identifying which components of the solution are most important.

One approach used to help stakeholders clarify and articulate their values is ***value stream mapping***, a technique developed in Lean manufacturing.

Value stream mapping analyzes, and potentially redesigns, the flow of materials and information required to deliver a product or service to the customer in order to reduce the total time from beginning to end of the entire stream, without taking shortcuts at the expense of future opportunities.

While there are various permutations, the basic value stream mapping process consists of the following steps:

- ***Identify the Value Stream Target.*** The target is a particular product or service (sometimes a product or service group, family or category) where improvement can provide strategic and competitive advantage.
- ***Define the Current State.*** Identifying the current state of the value stream is accomplished by creating a "map" showing the current process. The map illustrates the productive steps and accompanying information inputs required to deliver the product or service. It also identifies unproductive steps such as lead time, delays, queuing time, or holds. For tangible products, the flow will show everything from acquiring the raw materials to customer receipt of the product. For intangible products, the flow will show the design concept to the launch of the service or delivery of the product, such as a financial instrument or software.
- ***Clarify the Current Opportunity.*** Opportunities to eliminate waste (e.g., waiting time, delays, queuing, or holds) and thereby raise customer satisfaction and enhance competitive advantage with faster delivery and better quality and fit are clarified by analyzing the current-state value stream map.
- ***Depict the Desired Future State.*** Once the current state has been properly analyzed, a desired future-state value stream map is documented. That map is then used to implement a plan to transform the current workflow into the desired future state.

In most widely used forms of value stream mapping, the value-adding steps are drawn horizontally across the middle of the map and the non-value-adding steps are drawn on vertical lines perpendicular to the value stream. This makes the value-added activities the focus of attention and the waste-type activities apparent as cross-purposed steps in the flow. It does not imply that the steps are not operationally necessary, only that if and when they can be minimized, it will not create a negative impact on customer value.

Value stream mapping is part of the recognized Six Sigma methodologies. While in the past, value stream mapping was most often associated with manufacturing, it has begun to see widespread use in industries as varied as logistics, healthcare, and software development for establishing value-driven delivery processes.

Value stream mapping can also be linked to high-level architectural outlines. Such outlines may be needed to facilitate planning for the initial Iteration (aka "Just Enough"), guide architectural and engineering activities during subsequent Iterations (aka "Just In Time"), and meet any regulatory requirements (aka "Just Because"). Architectural outlines must be adequate to guide emergent design and incremental delivery of business value.

The test of value-driven deliverables is whether the releasable product reflects the product vision and meets the acceptance criteria (and related metrics) defined by the customer/proxy. Ultimately, however, it is customer adoption and usage that determines the true value of the project.

The theory of value-driven delivery is implemented through a practice called Backlog grooming.

H. Grooming the Backlog

If we use a UPS delivery person as a metaphor, product backlog grooming is the "steering wheel" ensuring the "Agile truck" is headed in the right direction and stops to deliver packages at the right time and location. Backlog grooming is important because research indicates that, for example, the cost of a $250,000 IT development project can have a negative variance of as much as $130,000 to achieve targeted functionality. The amount of the variance correlates to the maturity of the requirements. Because backlog grooming continuously improves project requirements, it has a direct, quantitative, positive financial impact.

Backlog grooming is a process that prioritizes and clarifies backlog items as it moves from the long-range edge of the time horizon into the current time horizon.

Backlog items typically start with descriptions with large, low resolution identifiers of capabilities, functions or features. As they move through the grooming process, from names on the Central Feature List, to stories with affinity estimates on the Roadmap, to Release plans with story point sizes, to Iteration plans with detailed estimates, they are refined by the customer's insight and learning generated by discussions with the team.

The information about each specific backlog item increases as it nears likely development. Grooming avoids waste by only gathering detailed information as it is needed and usable. Because most items will change, some of them quite dramatically, as development progresses and the customer/proxy gains insight, any resources spent on premature efforts to expand detailed information have a high probability of ending up as waste.

Overall, the backlog grows with time as more detailed information and new items are added. Because the quantity of backlog items, by definition, always exceeds the budget to deliver them, the process of grooming the backlog to align development decisions to business priorities and articulate them in Roadmaps and Release Plans, will always be significant.

APM leaders must ensure the customer/proxy is continuously refining the business value assessment of the product and setting backlog priorities accordingly. Although responsibility for the business value assessment lies primarily with the customer/proxy, APM leaders need to be capable of articulating in customer-facing, non-technical terms, the cost/benefit facets of the choices they must make.

Setting priorities drives product backlog grooming. The customer/proxy will lead customer collaboration activities such as focus groups, marketing studies, and product visioning exercises. Using those experiences, the customer/proxy will discern the timing and MMF set needed to create both incremental and long-term value.

The backlog is the tangible expression of the product vision and grooming is a real-time, rolling wave, Iterative process guiding the project through an evolutionary requirements elaboration process.

As organizations mature, a common practice is to use a Roadmap with the backlog defined at the capability level on the six month to multi-year horizon, Release plans with multiple or rolling three-month time horizons, and Iteration plans with one to four week time horizons at the story level.

A best practice for identifying and defining backlog items is to have the customer/proxy discuss each of the following elements with the team.

- Process elements – The definition, usage, and management of procedures discussed in the Business Case and Value Stream Map.
- Organizational elements – The infrastructure support for the current business practices and the support needs that must be developed for the future-state practices.
- Human elements – The knowledge and skills applied by the users in the current business practices and the additional user training needs for the future-state practices.
- Risk and Regulatory Compliance elements – What provisions are needed "just because" of the need for risk mitigation or regulatory compliance?
- Automation and Technology elements – How will the organization's approach to fulfilling required value-creation processes use a different model, such as queries replacing reports, pull replacing push inventory management, or automated replies replacing manual responses?

Because there are enormous differences between developing tangible and intangible products, as well as between large capital and product-to-market projects, the process of analyzing needs and defining features varies widely. However, elaboration processes should use a hierarchy, such as product, segment, and niche, or application, capability, and story, to help maintain structural coherence.

The lack of good release planning is rampant in parts of the Agile community who reject it as unnecessary. ***The Scrum Guide,*** the official Scrum rulebook maintained by Scrum.org, states that release planning is entirely optional. It then goes on to say that starting work without release planning artifacts will create impediments to resolve. It seems many Agile practitioners see the "entirely optional" part of that statement and miss the serious warning following it. Teams can get caught up in an Iteration-plus-backlog-only mindset and not invest in the planning needed for an entire release or project.

Doing this is a mistake because the teams can't adequately address significant business questions like, "How much will the total solution cost?" or "Will we have a releasable product on the launch date?" This lack of sensible answers creates immense frustration for the executives subjected to this behavior by Agile teams.

For Agile Project Management to succeed, it must use time boxes intelligently and well. When organizations transition to an Agile framework they still need – and demand – to accurately predict planned release dates. Customers simply won't accept anything less. So grooming backlogs and planning Roadmaps, Releases, and Iterations is part of a bigger process goal. The goal is to transform a product vision into a product backlog of features able to be estimated then measured to predictable points in time for delivering Releases.

There are two major approaches to the Agile planning process – planning by date or planning by scope. It is good to note the "or" in the prior sentence is not an "and" because many project failures have been induced by management who thought they could control both!

Planning by date means the release date is defined and the final list of specific features that will be in the release can be adapted as the reality of development occurs.

Planning by scope means that the MMF are defined first and a release date is calculated second. In situations where the release date is beyond an acceptable point in time, the MMF is reduced and a new release date is calculated. This cycle is repeated until an acceptable alternative is identified.

As explained earlier, reducing waste is a Lean principle imbedded in Agile frameworks. The frequency and level of detail in estimates must be tied to the business benefits of doing so. Elaboration for the sake of elaborating, or estimating for the sake of estimating, is waste. Elaborating and estimating to create insight, plan the future, and guide execution to create business value is not waste.

Because user stories can have a one-to-many relationship with tasks, some teams will choose to have stories in the backlog, but more detailed tasks in the other columns. When they do this, some teams include numbering or color-coding to identify the task to the story or person doing the work. Other teams use nested naming conventions and initials on the in-process tasks. The key is to create visibility into work that is being finished and what has been selected to work on next, by whom.

Electronic task boards for remote, distributed, and virtual teams accomplish the same purpose as their physical counterparts, and can often be facilitated using a conference call and a spreadsheet. Typically the task list – i.e., task board – is maintained on one tab and the estimate values are summarized and graphed on a second tab. The results can then be easily published as a daily PDF, printed and posted in each remote location, and archived for future reference.

Of course, to have any value at all, the reports must contain accurate, useful data, which implies reliance on another Agile concept, Osmotic communication.

I. Leveraging Osmotic Communication

The Agile ethos requires teams be cross-functional, self-directed, and trusted. It also recognizes that whenever possible, teams should be co-located in order to optimize the chance to identify risks and reduce errors. The team's osmotic communication about risks will dramatically affect the success of the project.

Osmotic communication means team members pick up pieces of information from conversations occurring near them and link that information to insights they can contribute to the discussion. The name is drawn from the perception that the relevant information was acquired in a fashion similar to minerals dissolving into a solution by osmosis.

It is worth noting that osmotic communication is a critical type of collaboration, significantly more complex than mere coordination or synchronization. Coordination can be achieved with a 15-minute daily meeting or a periodic conference call. Collaboration requires significantly more time and bandwidth that is often only available when teams are co-located.

Osmotic communication is powerfully effective and does not occur automatically or by accident. It must be cultivated.

Face-to-face is widely recognized as the most effective communication channel available and therefore is a core element of Agile Project Management. Osmotic communication is the expression of this truth. APM acknowledges that projects benefit when people with a high need to communicate are in close proximity where they can overhear communications between all parties. This heightens awareness of issues that are current and important so they can be responded to quickly.

The key implication is that team members should be co-located to take advantage of the improved information flow. There is an opportunity cost associated with team members not asking questions. When a team is co-located, their very proximity leads them to ask more questions and discover unexpected answers. Direct communication lowers the cost of information transfer and ultimately saves time!

This principle has been applied in Traditional Project Management for many decades when critical projects become troubled. In those cases, the common and best practice was, and still is, to create a "war room" and co-locate all the needed experts to rescue the project or address the threat. In fact, in the 1995 docudrama film about Apollo 13, a NASA mission to the moon where it appeared the astronauts might die of suffocation because a liquid oxygen tank exploded unexpectedly, crippling the spacecraft and robbing the astronauts of precious air. The power of the film pivoted on the real-life tension that existed as Lead Flight Director, Gene Kranz tried to save them. To find a workable solution for this critical, highly complex problem with the limited resources in the space capsule, he co-located the team in a war room and rallied them to get the astronauts home safely, declaring, "Failure is not an option!" Because the team included all the needed experts, despite the time pressure and constrained resources, a solution was found and the astronauts were saved.

Osmotic communication and collocation collocation are not without some limitations however. Foremost among those limits is team size. Both concepts work best with relatively small teams, but that can be a problem if a large project is involved. The next limitation is personal needs and preferences when doing tasks requiring serious, unbroken concentration. A best practice for mitigating this challenge is the concept of workspace design called caves and common room. Lastly is the need for occasional privacy to handle personal affairs and to sometimes just get away from "the noise".

The forgoing does not mean that Agile denies the reality that many projects are delivered by distributed teams. Instead, it recognizes the challenges and risks associated with teams that cannot attain the high trust levels fostered by collocation. The Agile Project Leader must develop operational practices for curbing the deterioration experienced by distributed teams in order to help them achieve the best level of communication possible.

Osmotic communication is just one of the key elements that must be addressed in order to cultivate Agile leadership.

J. Cultivating Agile Leadership

For this section, we will use a grossly over-simplified characterization to contrast leadership in Traditional and Agile environments. We acknowledge that it carries all of the drawbacks of any characterization, but it is helpful with comparing and contrasting the two approaches.

In the Traditional environment, the Project Manager often utilizes directive, command-and-control tactics, such as assigning tasks to team members to administer the project. By way of contrast, the Agile Project Leader relies on the team to achieve the project objectives. The dichotomy mirrors the old adage to lead people and manage things. The Traditional Project Manager addresses the tasks, milestones and dates in the plan to control change and pursue outcomes. The Agile Project Leader pursues outcomes by influencing the team as it embraces ambiguity and change. Both approaches have as their goal, to deliver results effectively, but each is based on a very different set of assumptions, commonly referred to as servant leadership in APM.

Servant leadership is a philosophy emphasizing awareness, listening, persuasion, relationship building, and commitment to others' growth, as the path to creating value. Servant leadership is embodied in practices such as embracing the energy and intelligence of others, developing colleagues, influencing teams, and inverting the power-pyramid.

One easily identifiable metric of how well an Agile Project Leader embodies servant leadership is the existence of an environment of personal safety.

Personal safety, as described by Alistair Cockburn, a well-known and respected Agile thought leader and author, is when team members feel supported as they work through the productive tension and respectful disagreements that accompany developing solutions to complex problems when uncertainty is unavoidable.

Being a servant leader and cultivating an environment of personal safety requires the Agile Project Leader develop a capability commonly described as emotional intelligence.

Emotional intelligence is the ability to identify, assess, and manage one's own emotions, and also the ability to identify, assess, and influence the emotions of others.

Jim Highsmith, another well-known and respected Agile thought leader and author, points out, "Management research shows that mood or "emotional intelligence" in leaders has a much larger impact on performance than we may have imagined." Thus, it is important for an Agile Project Leader not to be distracted by the use of a term that has become a cliché and instead, embrace the important issue it addresses.

Because the team will experience both highs and lows, quite often with unexpected volatility, during the project, supporting appropriate responses and discouraging inappropriate ones is critical. Being able to induce group dynamics conducive to creating desirable, emergent results at the edge of chaos where most teams must work is as fundamental to producing optimal results as writing good user stories. Therefore, the Agile Project Leader must recognize that their emotional intelligence will dramatically impact the team's success and take the steps needed to refine and improve it.

Agile Project Leaders help create an environment where emotional intelligence can flourish by applying the best practice of defining the team's rules of engagement.

Rules of engagement establish norms and expectations for team member interactions and are sometimes referred to as ground rules.

By demonstrating that the treatment of one another is an important area for the team to discuss, develop, and define, the Agile Project Leader can guide the team to document common expectations and assumptions so misunderstandings are avoided. By posting the rules in a prominent place to act as a reminder, the Agile Project Leader supports interdependent accountability even as the rules are adapted over time to improve team self-discipline.

The rules foster and direct the healthy and necessary contention of emergent design in positive ways. Great teams feed on the energy of diverse ideas in contention to produce the highest quality results. At the same time, they need positive guidance to avoid accidental negative interactions.

Examples of common Rules of Engagement include:

- Everyone participates
- Respect differences
- Attack issues, not people
- Everyone has an equal voice
- Everyone has a valuable contribution to make
- Honor confidentiality and privacy within the team

Cultivating an Agile team spirit excites productivity. It does so in part because the healthy contention of emergent design brings important risks into focus so the team can mitigate and resolve them.

Servant leadership relies on a number of skills and techniques, all aimed at developing and facilitating the Agile project team. They include:

- Mentoring team members on the Agile framework as well as on general management and technical skills.
- Allowing the cross-functional team to become self-directed and fully accountable.
- Facilitating team meetings including release planning, daily stand-ups, demonstrations, reflection workshops, reviews, and retrospectives.
- Guiding the team as they foster appropriate value-based decisions.
- Removing obstacles impeding progress, or facilitating the team to do so.

As the Agile team matures, it moves along a continuum from being a highly directed Traditional team to a self-organizing, cross-functional, highly motivated team. When they reach this state, the Agile Project Leader can largely act as a consultant, serving as a facilitator when called upon.

A best practice is for the Agile Project Leader is to avoid conducting individual performance reviews for members of the team as this creates a conflicting frame of reference for the team members and the appearance of violating the servant leadership role.

Another valuable thing to remember is that co-located teams enjoy a host of communication advantages and require only normal levels of support, whereas there is a very real challenge in supporting communication for virtual teams. That challenge is part of Agile leadership.

Key factors that must be considered include:

- Synchronizing communication
- Enabling collaboration
- Providing enough communication bandwidth

Remember that the foremost purpose of the daily meeting is to synchronize the team's work, requiring clear communication. The most common challenges for virtual teams are language and accent issues due to the lack of visual clues. Because so much communication is non-verbal, the lack of visual clues creates a huge risk of misunderstanding.

Two solutions to this challenge are available. First, invest in a good headset because vocal clues are very subtle. Second, establish a Rule of Engagement stating each team member will provide detailed written answers to the three questions preceding the call. Because English is the lingua franca of many business teams, but not everyone has a good "ear" for hearing past the accents of those speaking English as a second language, having a rule that each team member will start by reading their written answers to the three questions, they allow other teammates to follow along and develop an "ear" for the spoken word.

This simple practice vastly increases the quality of communication. It is a "trick" shared by Karen Schneider, who manages global projects and teams for IBM and is a long-time leader in the PMI – San Diego community.

Another key challenge working against enabling collaboration is time zones. There are many ways to deal with this issue including shifting core hours to find an overlap and using asynchronous communication like e-mails and wikis. A proven best practice is to modularize using a development hierarchy that distributes project-level pieces first, theme-level pieces second, team-level pieces third, followed by feature-level pieces, and lastly, function-level pieces (i.e., Developers, QA, Testers, etc.).

Providing enough communication bandwidth to achieve actual knowledge sharing is also a challenge. Solutions to this challenge include rotating developers across projects, features, and modules, using groupware tools like blogs and wikis, and investing in commercial Agile Project Management tools.

Whatever tools or techniques are used, it is a primary responsibility for the Agile Project Leader to ensure that true collaboration – not just coordination – occurs. That means participatory decision-making is critical.

K. Employing Participatory Decision-Making

Agile leaders seeking to optimize team performance need to use a participatory decision-making model in order to make sure each team member's voice is heard.

Participatory decision-making is a creative process where finding effective options is the purpose and ownership of decisions belongs to the team so everyone can support those decisions.

Over the last ten years, APM frameworks have enjoyed a meteoric rise in interest because of the way they improved operating outcomes for so many organizations. One of the variables easily identified as a significant contributor to that success is participatory decision making. The Agile ethos recognizes that simply having human beings act like biological machines cannot solve the significant, complex problems faced by most organizations. Organizations need the creative, non-linear, and imaginative insights that only come from fully engaged people.

Consider these two questions. Who is best qualified and most responsible for the solution best meeting the customer's needs? Is it best to have management interpret the customer's needs and act as an intermediary for the team doing the work or for the team to communicate directly with the customer?

Agile suggests the answer to both is the knowledge workers currently delivering results in today's organizations.

Knowledge workers are persons who combine various forms of structured and unstructured data and use creative thinking to solve mostly non-routine problems. They are commonly described as thinking for a living and include engineers, architects, scientists, lawyers, and Project Managers.

Today's knowledge workers are continuously dealing with environmental challenges in order to understand how to solve the problem from the viewpoint of production. In APM, the process is dynamic, always changing to meet an evolving challenge, as the team moves through the Cone of Uncertainty.

In 1999, Peter Drucker, the world-renown business management consultant and author, emphasized the need for organizations to empower the knowledge worker to make decisions that they – more so than management – are in the best position to make; and also to avoid having the knowledge workers leave, damaging the organization. In Jim Collins's famous book, *Good to Great*, an outline of the answer is also identified. The great organizations he described engage in rigorous debate, often over extended periods of time, using dialogue, not coercion, to interrogate the truth down to the brutal facts, in a way allowing individuals to be extremely interactive, until the best solution is identified. We also see it implied in Roger Martin's article, *The Opposable Mind: How Successful Leaders Win Through Integrative Thinking*, where he describes how real leaders, great leaders, tolerate and embrace ambiguity, as long as necessary, during discussion because they refuse to be limited by "either/or" choices.

The Agile methodology and its many frameworks have embraced participatory decision.

Because the quality of the solution delivered by an Agile team is based on the trust and respect needed to enable a free flow of information, vigorous discussions and active participation by every member, the participatory decision-making process is engaged and fostered to maturity in the Agile ethos. Experience has shown that if any of those key components is left out, ineffective, poor quality results follow. Experience has also shown that it is difficult to develop the sophisticated leadership skill needed to facilitate, influence, and coach a team into the healthy, durable relationships required for participatory decision making.

Participatory decision-making either helps the team operate smoothly or mires it in a swamp of indecision. The difference is largely dependent on the actions of the leader. If the leader shies away from the discussion necessary to get the structural engineer to challenge the architect, then the building can't be built cost-effectively. If the construction manager has to attend too many meetings in the name of "coordination", the project gets hopelessly behind schedule because the team doesn't have access to the customer/proxy when needed. The ends of the continuum – too little and too much – can both cripple participatory decision-making.

Leadership is critical to effective decision making in an Agile project environment where thousands of decisions must be made using information that is often vague. Customer desires are unclear. Technology is untried in the exact situation. Eight out of ten decisions can paralyze the team because the fuzziness makes them oscillate between choices. Often times, once the required, healthy, vigorous debate has occurred and the team has reached an impasse because the ambiguity engulfs them, the leader has to step forward. An effective leader acknowledges the ambiguity, takes responsibility for the impact of the decision – whatever it may be – and enables the team to resume productivity by making the decision.

The basic assumption of participatory decision-making is that the right team is executing the project.

L. Acquiring the Right Team

It seems necessary to reiterate that APM is not a magic potion or a silver bullet because many Agile evangelists act as if it is. Without the right skills on a team, nothing can help, not even APM. So the Agile Project Leader's question is not, "Can we please have a cross-functional team with the right skills?" The Agile Project Leader must communicate that it is not optional to have a cross-functional team with the right skills. Therefore question really is, "How do we go about getting that particular team?"

The first part of the answer is actually a reality check. If the project is number 103 on the company's priority list, the Agile Project Leader must frame the team requirements within that reality. The crucial key is to use the Business Case and Flexibility Matrix, described above, to solicit the level of sponsorship needed to clarify the tactical reality with the customer/proxy.

The second part of getting the particular team the project needs requires evaluating potential (or assigned) team members according to key factors such as:

- Ability – What specific competencies do they provide?

- Availability – What is their availability and what are their competing commitments? Are they local or remote?
- Cost – How appropriate is their cost given the budget constraint?
- Chemistry – How well do their work style preferences align with the team culture and environment?
- Experience – What similar or related work have they done? Under what time and quality constraints?

In many, if not most organizations, whether using a Traditional or Agile framework, one of the biggest challenges to getting the proper team is pre-assignment.

Pre-assignment means that someone in the organization, without the Agile Project Leader's involvement, has allocated, appointed, or designated some or all of the specific persons who will make up the team.

Pre-assignment is a common practice in large organizations and helps when the project is dependent on specific expertise in short supply. Sometimes pre-assignment involves specific individuals who were identified as a part of contract negotiation and so must be honored. But pre-assignment also happens many other times when there is limited rationale for the Agile Project Leader accepting it. In those circumstances, the Agile Project Leader must carefully evaluate whether critical skills are missing from the team and take steps to correct the problem.

It may also be necessary for the Agile Project Leader to act in order to ensure the project receives competent staff on a timely basis and team members don't have their bandwidth constricted due to new work assignments. A professional Agile Project Leader must be willing and able to negotiate as toughly as required to ensure project success.

The desired result is the right person in the right role at the right time. Until the team has that result, the Agile Project Leader must continue to negotiate and secure those people for the project team.

With the right team in place and the project rolling, it is time to look towards continuous improvement.

M. Benefitting from Continuous Improvement

APM uses continuous improvement to expand the Agile framework from a focus on the team's performance (i.e., micro-dynamic) to improving the entire development environment (i.e., macro-dynamic). Doing so has the benefit of addressing problems bigger than the team. Value stream mapping applies the Lean principle of optimizing the whole by identifying waste, such as rework and late problem detection, and correlating it to root causes, such as multi-tasking and overloading the team.

Continuous improvement is the ongoing practice of advancement through incremental or disruptive changes to the design of the delivery process increasing efficiency, effectiveness and flexibility. W. Edwards Deming pioneered this idea as part of the systems thinking used in the Toyota Production System.

This requires investing effort and resources to move from an existing baseline to a more desirable level of functioning. It seeks incremental change over time, which is the Agile best practice, or breakthrough change, as is the case in other settings.

Agile frameworks intend to deliver the right product for the current need, which may be different than the need that existed when the project began. Therefore, Agile teams must be open to, and embrace, the emerging changes as they move forward. In APM frameworks, backlog grooming is a business-level, continuous improvement process while retrospective meetings are a team-level, continuous improvement process.

The Agile Project Leader must have the wisdom to help the team define the metrics, the discipline to track performance against those metrics, and the skill to help the team understand, evaluate and apply that information in order to create a pattern of continuous improvement.

CHAPTER

3

Basis for Agile Government Contracting Methods

You may not believe it, but Agile Government Contracting is not new, even if the energized drive to apply the concepts to every Department, Command, Agency, and User Community is.

Since the 1950s, both National Aeronautics and Space Administration (NASA) and the DoD have been using iterative and incremental development approaches to deliver significant program results. When done correctly, they enable flexibility and control by making decisions based on the concrete data from working, tested prototypes of the solution. The idea of creating prototypes and testing them early creates an environment where major design flaws can be found and fixed without requiring significant change orders, substantial rework, or implementation of options with risky performance/cost profiles.

Agile Government Contracting got a big push forward in March 2009 when the DoD Defense Science Board Task Force published their report, ***"DoD Policies and Procedures for the Acquisition of Information Technology".*** It described what was hailed as a "new" model at the time and has gone on to see many extensions and applications since then.

A. DoD Defense Science Board Model

Because the field of information technology, by its very nature, means procurements occur in a complex and highly uncertain environment, it has been an incubator of Agile acquisition and Project Management tools, techniques and best practices.

Therefore, as a baseline we will describe the model proposed by the Defense Science Board Task Force here then enhance and detail specific variations, additions, processes and procedures in the rest of this field guide.

Agile Government contracting has unique characteristics, driven by shorter timeframes and evolving capability requirements, designed to produce transformational results in an environment of evolving best practices, processes, and organizational structures.

Any model tailored to such an environment must be steadfast in its focus to reduce waste and increase value-added activities through a combination of enhanced stakeholder engagement and analytical rigor during the entire procurement and program.

Every successful model will include proven fundamentals, such as:

- Comprehensive user involvement.
- Appropriately-executed, short, developmental increments that deliver well-defined Releases of functionality.
- Early prototyping supporting an emergent design engineering approach focused on modular, open-systems architecture for future operations and support.
- Commands, Agencies, and User Communities that are properly trained to participate in their newly defined roles, before, during and after development.

Model Characteristics

The Defense Science Board Model has four phases:

Phase 1. Business Case Analysis and Development

This phase produces an Initial Capability Document (ICD) defining the specific needs of the agency, warfighter, or user, and the required capabilities of possible solutions.

Phase 2. Architectural Development and Risk Reduction

This phase produces defined, high-level, architectural guidelines for significant core features, followed by prototype and testing metrics that validate the viability and cost/performance trade-offs of various technologies. Development includes prototypes and lab-testing as needed and appropriate. This process leads to increased understanding of user needs, and refined expectations regarding capabilities so prioritized choices can be made to minimize high-risk features while simultaneously improving cost/performance trade-offs.

Phase 3. Development and Demonstration

Phase 3 produces prioritized operational capabilities that are built and delivered in discrete Releases, or "chunks", according to baseline plans at the sub-program level. Development includes field-testing in appropriate environments and training programs, as needed, to ensure an accurate assessment of the probability of successfully deploying the new capabilities within the defined user population.

Phase 4. Operations and Support

This phase produces material readiness, scalable user training, and validated operational support programs for the life-cycle of the solution.

This model (see Figure 3.1) is intended to deliver superior acquisition results to overcome the, sometimes spectacular, failures of the past caused by not including enough architectural analysis and systems engineering rigor within the program. In the past, some acquisitions served specific DoD commands or agencies well, but failed to align with needed enterprise processes or controls.

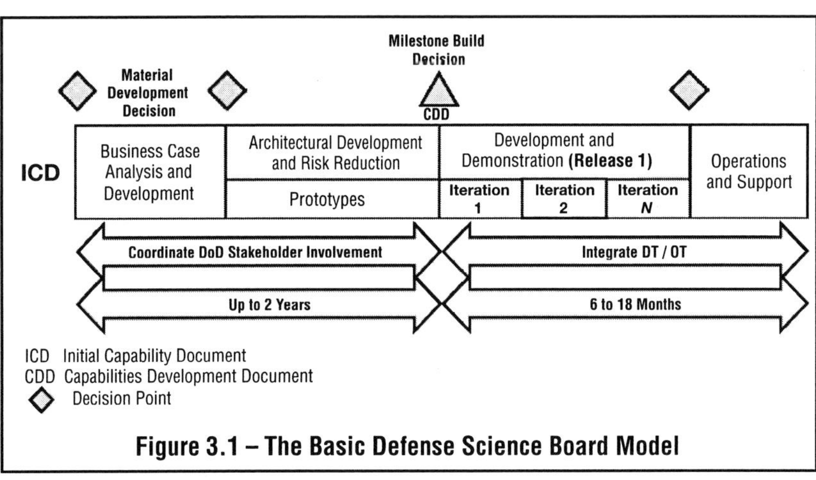

Figure 3.1 – The Basic Defense Science Board Model

The Defense Science Board Model creates a program initiation process, starting with a credible business case, where analytical discipline supports program- and enterprise-level outcomes. The business case demonstrates and balances the unique needs of the sponsoring DoD Command or Agency with the added-value of larger enterprise goals, when appropriate.

The goal is to integrate the mission-specific objectives of the procurement or program while avoiding the redundancy and inefficiency that inevitably occurs when enterprise-level guidance is not considered.

Extensive research and experience have shown that models where proper up-front analysis occurs – when requirements have the most flexibility – can avoid potentially significant rework costs later. They can also best balance the unavoidable trade-offs between local and enterprise-based decision-making and best optimize procurement results.

Requirements have the most flexibility and least change-related costs before development and production. Remember the Cone of Uncertainty? The impact and cost of changes goes up as the program approaches "certainty." Agile uses up-front planning to balance trade-offs, avoid costs, and optimize results.

Tactically, the process includes appropriate prototyping and testing of each developmental increment to ensure the solution functionality can realistically be delivered, while offering the optimum performance/cost trade-off, as shown in Figure 3.2.

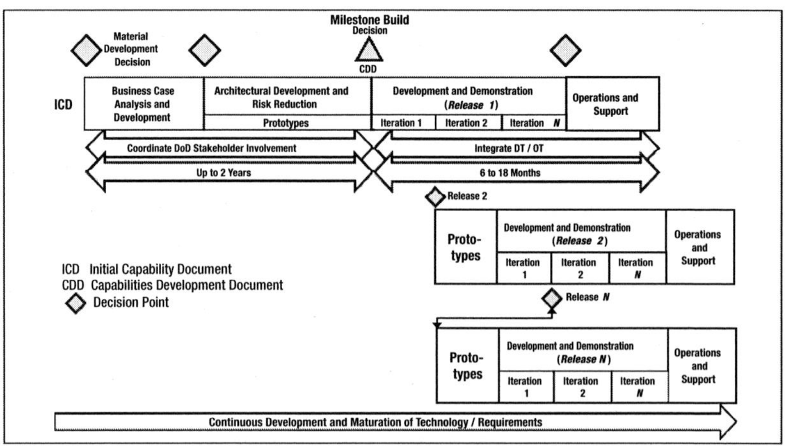

Figure 3.2 – The complete Defense Science Board Model

Successfully prototyping and testing in-the-field capabilities implies that appropriate documentation, user training, and system and user support is concurrently developed. All of which must be built on a foundation of strong user feedback, both early and throughout, development.

The Federal Acquisition Institute, who has civilian Government project and program oversight responsibilities similar to Defense Acquisition University for the DoD, is implementing a certification regimen that is life-cycle based. It will use the same set of life-cycle phases that are being used by the Department of Veteran Affairs, the largest federal civilian agency.

As Figure 3.3 shows, those phases are Concept Definition, Concept Planning, Development, Implementation, Operations and Maintenance, and Closeout.

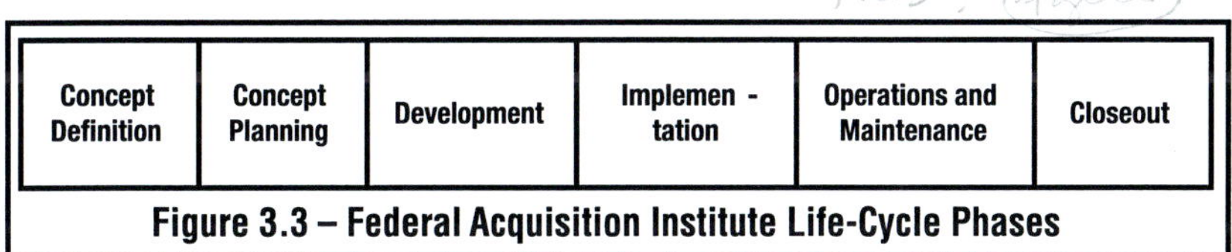

Concept Definition	Concept Planning	Development	Implemen - tation	Operations and Maintenance	Closeout

Figure 3.3 – Federal Acquisition Institute Life-Cycle Phases

It also includes the Business Case concept as described in ***OMB Exhibit 300*** in the phases.

All of these models – iterative development models – include certain characteristics new to many DoD Command and Agency professionals. For example the models include:

- A single, approved Capability Development Document (CDD), typically fully funded, but delivered in multiple Releases of functionality.
- Releases that have been subsequently divided into multiple, rapidly-executed Iterations to facilitate development where progress – not just cost, effort, or time spent – can be assessed according to the prioritized scope of work.
- Iterations where actual, potentially-deployable, functionality can be tested for both user acceptance and integration into defined enterprise capabilities.
- Enterprise and program capabilities continuing to evolve (within the limits of the approved CDD) and leverage what is being learned during the Iterations and Releases.

- Shorter development cycles resulting in something less than the complete envisioned capability – a change the DoD Command or Agency must be prepared to accept – en route to the final goal. This is also sometimes referred to "evolutionary acquisition."
- Smaller acquisitions using fewer resources, are competed more frequently, and involve simpler, open-source technologies. Rather than build one large, lumbering, proprietary-laden mega-contract – COs and PMs can focus on smaller, interoperable requirements and contracts. These smaller contracts are more effective, easier to administer, and are more responsive to the customer needs. They are also more often awarded to small businesses, giving them added benefit over these multiple award, mega-contracts because they help the Federal Government reach closer to the goal of awarding 23% of all federal dollars to small business. Note: this goal is historically and consistently illusive.
- Contract vehicles allowing enough flexibility for changes during increments by deferring specific capabilities to subsequent increments, avoiding onerous cost consequences to the Government.

Operationally, the objective of the model is to develop and deploy mission capabilities with the highest priority in each Iteration. Then, continuously work through the scope, developing the lower priority capabilities. That means the capabilities in the CDD must be prioritized by mission objectives and delivered in increments with active user engagement. Then, as the results of development and testing become known, appropriate re-prioritization of requirements and functionality must be done to prevent delays and support rapid, iterative development and deployment of the next highest priority.

More reliable cost estimates are a significant benefit of this type of model. By managing the acquisition with well-defined units demonstrating actual progress – not just effort or time spent – realistic cost and schedule baselines can be created and maintained. Also, properly defined iterative projects have a tight alignment with Earned Value Management (EVM), as we will explain in the Chapter on EVM.

Because each Release or Iteration is procured and managed as a sub-project, cost and schedule estimating and reporting are independently driven and can be aggregated to reflect program results and performance against priority metrics.

That means that the contracting approach will require carefully defined increments of capability so the Program Manager can defer, or rearrange them, based on his or her expert judgment and authority. This approach is a challenge for companies to price – and for CO's to build a CLIN structure around. To define capabilities as options make sense if they are existing add-ons, such as the pre-priced options when buying a car. However, in the developmental arena, this may be more difficult to structure and price so the CO and Program Manager will have to maintain a high level of communication and mutual understanding.

This model requires COs and Program Managers to agree on fixed budgets and timelines while allowing the delivery of specific, defined capabilities to be rearranged within those constraints.

Industry experience has shown that leadership experience is vital for this type of procurement model, so contract award should require strong, relevant Contractor experience and a commitment that key Contractor personnel are committed in durable team formations for the duration of the project.

Additionally, the Contractor's development team must be skilled in, and required to use, standards-based models with well-defined and published interfaces, so the Government maintains an optimum range of vendor-selection choices for future development and system maintenance.

Using an Agile model, such as this, increases Government capability, reduces cost, and improves results, as demanded by the current environment.

B. Program and Project Managers (FAC-P/PM)

Whether the Command or Agency chooses to start with a generic model or the Defense Science Board Model, as described previously, it is critical that adequately skilled Program and Project Managers be involved in developing accurate Government requirements, defining measurable performance standards, and managing life-cycle activities to ensure that the intended procurement outcomes are achieved.

Therefore, it behooves Department, Command and Agency Leaders as well as COs to be aware of the one and only federal, civilian, *Government-wide* Project Management certification standard available today. The Federal Acquisition Certification for Program and Project Managers (FAC-P/PM) focuses on essential functional and technical competencies needed by Program and Project Managers. It applies a three-level competency-based certification beyond the *Project Management Institute, A Guide to the Project Management Body of Knowledge, (PMBOK Guide®) – Fifth Edition, Project Management Institute, Inc. 2012.*

Many agencies are putting certification programs in place to insure their personnel possess the FAC-P/PM in addition to agency-specific competencies.

C. Applying DoD Directive 5000.01

While we recognize the great divide between DoD and civilian agencies, and the need for caution when suggesting DoD practices might apply to civilian agencies, this section supports DoD procurements and may provide some possible insight for civilian agencies. Disregard it if it does not apply to your situation.

DoD Directive (DoDD) 5000.01 provides a specific, simplified, flexible management process for acquisitions that include weapon systems, services, and Automated Information Systems (AISs).

DoD Instruction (DoDI) 5000.02 provides the instructions for applying the DoDD.

It must be applied in a manner consistent with all statutory requirements and references, but authorizes Milestone Decision Authorities (MDAs), tailored to the regulatory information requirements and acquisition process to achieve cost, schedule, and performance goals.

Using the improved processes defined in DoD Directive 5000.02 is required:

- For the acquisition of new or replacement stand-alone IT

systems and subsystems and/or upgrading existing weapon systems' embedded IT components without changing the non-IT hardware.

- When many design trade-off decisions must be made for both hardware and IT systems, and/or for partitioning embedded IT systems' and subsystems' functionality and interoperability in a new system in order to ensure network compatibly and enterprise interoperability.

Using DOD Directive 5000.02 processes may be appropriate:

To acquire new embedded IT systems for a major weapon system acquisition when the existing IT technology will be several generations old at the time of Initial Operational Capability (IOC).

CHAPTER

4

Agile Fundamentals for Government Contracting

The principles of Lean Manufacturing, as developed and proven by the Toyota Production System, have revolutionized the productivity of many industries and organizations, inside and outside of manufacturing-specific contexts. Lean, as it is now commonly referred to, pivots on one core principle – ***eliminate waste!***

This core principle is simple to understand, but not easy to implement. Over the years, deploying Lean in all the various manufacturing and service industries it now influences has led to the creation of a great many broad and specific best practices, tools and techniques.

Lean principles have been used in environments as diverse as NASA, the U.S. Air Force's Air Logistics Centers, Qualcomm®, the communications giant, and Nike®, the consumer products legend.

It is now generally accepted wisdom that Lean can be applied to both tangible and intangible products and services to improve delivery time, reduce cost and improve quality simultaneously. While that claim may seem improbable or impossible, Lean delivers results using several basic, scientifically quantifiable principles.

Avoidable and Unavoidable Waste.

The first of those principles, noted above, is to eliminate waste whenever and wherever possible. Lean acknowledges that waste can be divided into two broad categories – avoidable and unavoidable. It attempts to eliminate all avoidable waste and minimize all unavoidable waste.

In Government contracting, the process of competition is supposed to be inefficient. The inherent goal of competing as many contracts on an "equal playing field" creates inefficiencies, repetition, and even re-competitions for the same work. However, to have an open Government market where many, or nearly any, company can compete, we must embrace a certain amount of un*avoidable waste.* To prove the point, would you want the US Government to give every aspect of some requirement to one contractor and just let them mange the whole thing? That would be efficient and would avoid waste (in theory), but it sure would not meet the intent of a capitalistic economy that is built on the value and innovation that comes from companies competing for work.

For example, a great deal of contractor support was needed when the US military invaded Iraq in 2003. Many contracts were awarded *without competition* for speed and *efficiency*. Companies like Halliburton, Bechtel and KBR received contracts outside the competitive process driven by the need for expediency to meet mission requirements. History now shows that while this approach made for an *efficient* award process, it also created a great deal of *avoidable waste.* Google these circumstances and decide for yourself.

The goal of this book is to demonstrate how COs and PMs can reduce *avoidable waste* (which may be the bigger portion by the way) by using Agile techniques instead of Traditional ones.

> **ONE KEY:** When developing requirements, focus on features the customer is *certain to use, first!*

Generally accepted wisdom states the greatest waste of all is developing and delivering all or any part of a product or service that the customer – the User – will not or does not use.

Interestingly, research first published and presented by Jim Johnson, Chairman, Standish Group International, Inc., at the XP2002 Conference in Sardinia, Italy, validated just how much waste actually exists in many IT projects. The research showed that only 20% of IT system features were used Always or Often, compared with a whopping 45% of features that were Never used, as shown in Figure 4.1.

While some of the features Users reported as "Never" used are unavoidable waste in the Lean lexicon because they serve other purposes such as security or regulatory compliance, clearly some of the

FEATURE USAGE

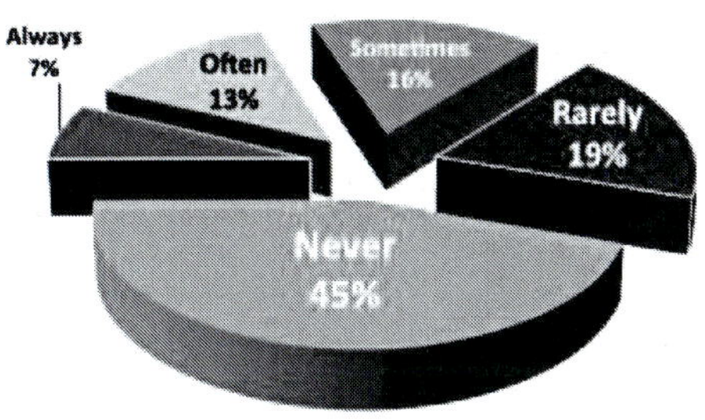

Feature Usage reported by Jim Johnson, Chairman, Standish Group Int'l, Inc.
XP2002 Conference, Sardinia, Italy

Figure 4.1 – Standish Group Research

"Never" features fall into the avoidable waste category. Consider that if just one-third of the Never features were avoidable, the system could have been delivered, theoretically, 15% faster and cheaper, and would be 15% better in terms of reduced Total Cost of Ownership (TCO) and life-cycle support metrics. While there is no way of knowing what the development cost or time for the Never used features was, they could have been cheap and easy or difficult and expensive, what is certain is that some measure of faster and cheaper development and reduced TCO and life-cycle support was possible.

Of course, one might argue that because the research only covered IT projects or that because it was done in 2002 it does not fairly portray today's reality. However, the exact opposite is more likely true. Every project today seems to have a significant IT component and has definitely become more complex and uncertain than it was in 2002. Considering the results of the research actually depict the symptoms exposing the underlying causes, it is more useful today than when it was first delivered.

A second principle of Lean, define the value the customer desires, is obviously applicable to Government procurements and programs whether the ultimate customer is a war fighter, fire fighter, or waste fighter. What's more, the process used in Lean and Agile Project Management to define customer value is based on bedrock scientific observations.

Millennia of human experience have shown that the farther into the future we attempt to peer, the more inexact, vague, and unreliable our perception gets. Other factors, such as complexity and uncertainty, amplify this inevitable effect of time as we peer into the future. So, regardless of how much time and money we choose to spend on creating highly precise descriptions and highly engineered estimates, it all proves to be part of the waste stream, as far as Lean is concerned, because it does not increase accuracy or reliability, which are the two core variables of customer value for planning activities.

A. Lean, Agile, and the PMBOK Guide®

The *PMBOK Guide®*, beginning with the section where it describes levels of estimating then integrating the section on progressive elaboration, lays out a cogent planning process where Lean concepts begin to emerge. The process aligns with the Defense Science Board Model and with Agile Project Management best practices.

The *PMBOK Guide®* describes three levels of estimating; Rough Order of Magnitude (ROM), Budgetary and Definitive. It states that each level has a corresponding degree of Design Completion and Accuracy. For ROM the degree of Design Completion is 0% to 10% and the expected estimating Accuracy level is +100% to -50%. For Budgetary, the degree of Design Completion is 15% to 25% and the expected estimating Accuracy level is +30% to -15%. And for Definitive, the degree of Design Completion is 45% to 100% and the expected estimating Accuracy level is +15% to -5%.

Those levels of Design Completion and expected estimating Accuracy can be correlated to an understanding of the unavoidable variances of future predictions due to the inescapable nature of time, as shown in Figure 4.2.

As Figure 4.2 demonstrates, the context of estimating and planning is an environment of uncertainty where variances are unavoidable. Even though estimates are typically expressed as a point, a single numerical value, they represent a range. The best, most mature estimators factor for complexity, effort and uncertainty, mentally establish a range, then propose the value-point best representing the range.

It is widely accepted that the farther into the future the work to be performed is, the wider the inescapable variance will be. But in every case, the variance is asynchronous because it is more likely to be underestimated than overestimated.

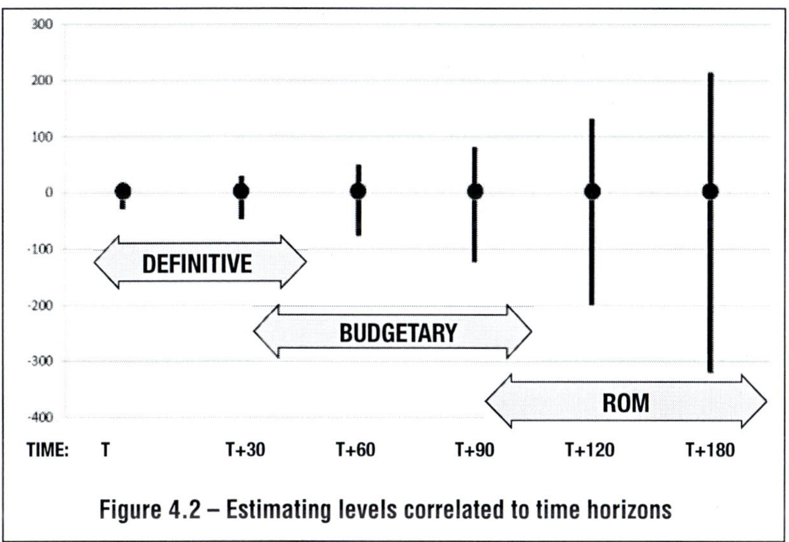

Figure 4.2 – Estimating levels correlated to time horizons

The only constant is that variance is unavoidable. That is so regardless of how much money and time is spent to increase the precision of the work description, assumptions, and calculations. All that can be accomplished with high-precision is an increase in the *avoidable* waste stream – the opposite of a well-defined Lean principle!

So the objective when the Defense Science Board Model or an APM framework is used is to reduce avoidable waste. Fulfilling that objective can best be understood by considering the Cone of Uncertainty.

B. The Cone of Uncertainty

Agile Project Management frameworks accept that developing and delivering solutions – procurements and programs – that solve complex problems is most efficiently accomplished in an environment of discovery and adaptation.

As Figure 4.3 shows, for a procurement or program to move from an initial understanding of a complex problem to a viable, effective solution – *by definition* – means that everyone involved, from the Command or Agency stakeholders, to the Contracting Officer and

Program Manager, to the development team Contractors, will have to move through an environment defined by uncertainty where discovery and adaptation is reality. No amount of effort spent on increasing precision will increase the planning and estimating accuracy that leads to the optimal solution. That does ***not*** mean adequate, responsible planning is impossible. It ***does*** mean that an iterative model, that is an Agile framework comparable to the Defense Science Board's model, is the intelligent process to apply.

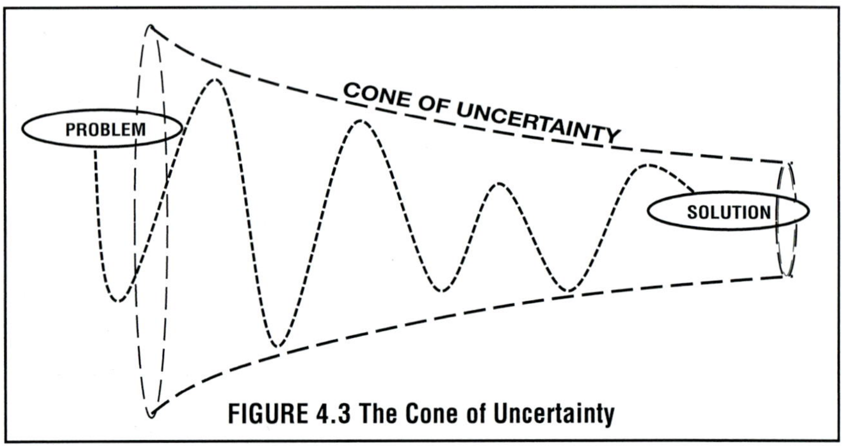

FIGURE 4.3 The Cone of Uncertainty

In contrast, consider the differences between the Traditional Project Management and the Agile Project Management paradigms for estimating, as shown in Figure 4.4.

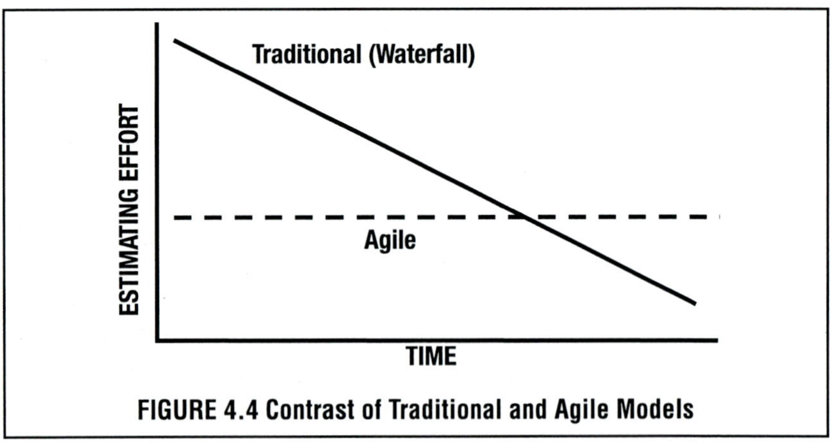

FIGURE 4.4 Contrast of Traditional and Agile Models

Over the years, in classes with hundreds of students, we have asked a very basic question, "When is it ***best*** to do ***detailed*** estimating; (a) when you know very little or (b) when you know a lot?" After a bit of confusion because the answer is so obvious students think it is a trick question, the universal response is that it is best to do estimating when more is known, not less! Yet, in the Traditional Model – as practiced by many Project Managers – the exact opposite happens. It violates both common sense and the practice of Rolling Wave Planning as described in the *PMBOK Guide®* to do detailed estimating and planning when little (or nothing!?) is really known. Given the high-uncertainty and high-complexity of any significant procurement or program, it is silly to spend precious, expensive resources on time-consuming work creating high-precision, detailed planning and estimating when there is not any corresponding increase in accuracy or reliability!

That is why Agile embraces the *PMBOK Guide®* and does Rolling Wave Planning by applying the proven common sense. For the near term time window, Agile implies Definitive estimates because the degree of Design Completion is between 45% and 100%, making estimating Accuracy between +15% and -5%. For the mid-term time window, Agile uses Budgetary estimates because the degree of Design Completion is only 15% to 25%, allowing estimating Accuracy to be between +30% and -15%. Finally, for the long-term time window, Agile uses ROM estimates because the degree of Design Completion is below 10%, prompting estimating Accuracy to fall between +100% and -50%.

The same logic can be applied to the Defense Science Board Model's four phases. During Phase 1, the Business Case Analysis and Development step, an ICD is produced defining the specific needs of the agency, warfighter, or user, and the required capabilities of possible solutions. No estimates are attempted because the degree of Design Completion is zero (0%). During Phase 2, the Architectural Development and Risk Reduction step, the degree of Design Completion is below 10% so the use of ROM estimates is correct. During Phase 3, the Development and Demonstration step, the degree of Design Completion is only 15% to 25% so Budgetary estimates are appropriate and feasible. Lastly, in Phase 4, the Operations and Support step, the degree of Design Completion is between 45% and 100%, so Definitive estimates should be required.

C. Planning Despite High-Complexity and High-Uncertainty

The PMBOK Guide® describes a proven, common sense approach to planning when it states that phases are sequenced as, "...beginning with an initial phase, followed by a series of intermediate phases, and ending in a final phase." What is often misunderstood is that the *The PMBOK Guide®* is agnostic, neutral or silent about what you call those phases or steps.

As Figure 4.5 demonstrates, whether the vocabulary from the *The PMBOK Guide®* is used, as shown in the top series, or any of the alternate terms are used, as shown in the bottom series, the objective of a final production deliverable is the result.

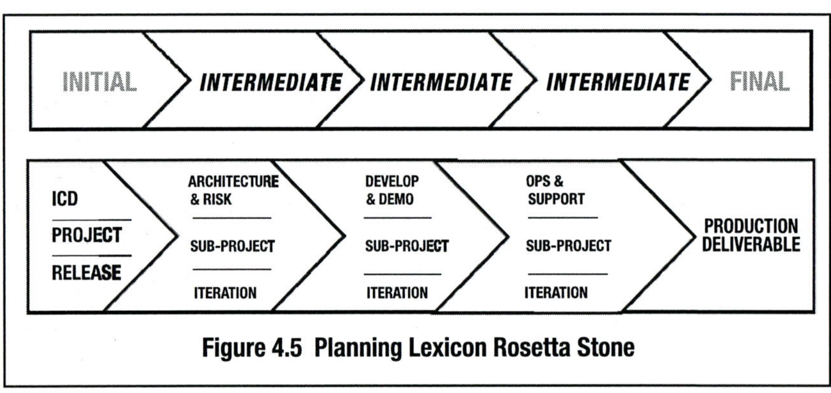

Figure 4.5 Planning Lexicon Rosetta Stone

In the bottom series, top thread, the process from ICD to Architecture & Risk to Develop & Demonstrate to Operations & Support leads to a final production deliverable. In the middle thread, the process from Project to a series of Sub-Projects leads to a final production deliverable. In the bottom thread, the process from Release to a series of Iterations leads to a final production deliverable. So regardless of the vocabulary chosen, a Rolling Wave, iterative planning process leads to the same desired solution.

Another way to understand this process is to consider it as a closed-loop, iterative planning and execution process. Figure 4.6 charts the flow of information, decisions, and deliverables from such a system.

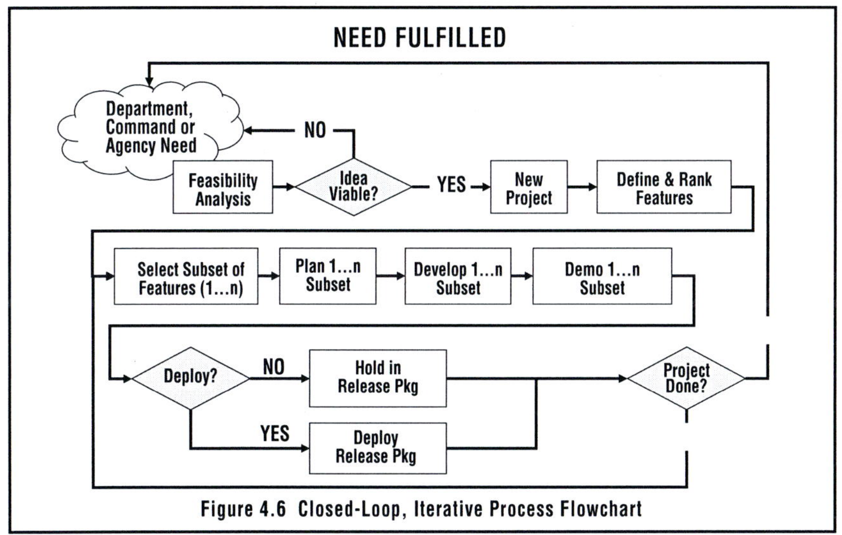

Figure 4.6 Closed-Loop, Iterative Process Flowchart

The process starts with the recognition of a Department, Command or Agency need that leads to a Feasibility Study. The first decision is whether or not the idea is viable. In other words, does it warrant the investment of resources to solve and does it appear it is reasonably solvable? Only if the answer to those questions is "Yes" does the process proceed and a new project is born.

Each new project must then use a process to Define and Rank, (prioritize) the Features that will provide the functionality needed to solve the problem. Once those features are defined and ranked, the highest priority Subset is selected for Planning, followed by Development and Demonstration. Those three steps – Plan, Develop, and Demo – are completed during each Iteration so progress can be measured.

At the end of each Iteration, the next decision is whether to Deploy the functionality demonstrated. If the answer is "No", the functionality is placed in a Hold or Interim Release environment. If the answer is "Yes", Deployment occurs.

A follow-on question is then asked. Is the Project done? If the answer is "No", the process returns to the Select step immediately preceding the Iteration. If the answer is "Yes", project close-out occurs and the process starts over again with the next need.

CHAPTER

5

Government-Approved Innovative Contracting Methods

New and revised contracting methods and procurement techniques are now available to Contracting Officers, Procurement Professionals and Project and Program Managers. Other methods in this book have been available for some time, but have been under-utilized. All of these options are needed in today's climate of changing priorities, budget cuts and realignments, and sweeping changes caused by sequestration.

Long-time Traditional tools like Invitations for Bids (IFBs), Requests for Quotes (RFQs) and Requests for Proposals (RFPs) offer opportunities for Agile techniques. In addition, the increasingly popular Federal Supply Schedules (FSS), Blanket Purchase Agreements (BPAs), BPAs under FSS contracts, Government-wide Agency Contracts (GWACS), and other multiple-award vehicles are innovative contracting techniques delivering better, faster, and more competitive procurements when used effectively with Agile in mind.

In order to drive down acquisition lead times, the DoD will need to continue embracing these Agile techniques. When COs and PMs combine Agile techniques with the commercial best practices, they create flexibility and remarkable results. The potential savings in time and money to both Government and industry (and the tax payer) are enormous.

These new and revised acquisition vehicles maximize Government flexibility by increasing real competition among suppliers with multiple award contracts and blanket purchasing agreements, further driving down price and driving up efficiency for commoditized products that Government buys in large quantities.

> **CO NOTE:** However, these large multiple award contracts (MACs) can be a slippery slope. The assumption that the economy of scale increases infinitely, without an impact on the quality of the goods or services and the associated cost of managing the contract as it grows, may be incorrect. We give examples of the perils of this 'overuse' of MACs in other parts of this book.

Applying these Agile techniques requires professionals on both the *contracting* and *contractor* sides to understand how to effectively use two fundamental concepts – Multiple Awards and Simplified Acquisition Procedures (SAP).

A. Multiple Awards

Multiple award procurements are founded on the concept of Indefinite-Delivery Indefinite-Quantity (IDIQ) contracts. IDIQ contracts enable Government purchases, within certain limits, of supplies or services during defined time periods, often without obligating the Government to purchase any more than a minimum specified amount.

For example, the General Services Administration's (GSA) approved Multiple Award Schedules / Federal Supply Schedule (MAS/FSS) approach awards IDIQ contracts to multiple Contractors or companies for comparable products.

This approach maximizes the Government's flexibility by only placing orders after an actual need is recognized, limiting the Government's legal obligation to appropriate minimums as specified in the contract, and enabling order placement using electronic media.

Importantly, GSA is now using the FSS to provide services, such as engineering, environmental management, marketing, media, and public relations.

The Government utilizes three types of indefinite-delivery contracts.

- ***FAR 16.502 – Indefinite-Delivery, Definite-Quantity***
- ***FAR 16.503 – Indefinite-Delivery-Requirements***
- ***FAR 16.504 – Indefinite-Delivery, Indefinite-Quantity***

These contract types are utilized when the Government cannot identify the exact time and/or quantity of future deliveries when the contract award is made. For more information on IDIQ's, see Chapter 6.

FAR subpart 8.4 (Federal Supply Schedules) details the procedures that apply to Government agencies when placing orders with individual FSS Contracts. ***FAR Part 38*** (Federal Supply Schedule Contracting) briefly discusses the fact that the GSA is solely responsible for establishing FSS contracts.

Blanket Purchase Agreements under FAR Part 8

FAR 8.405-3 governs BPAs established against FSS. It states that BPAs may be established under any schedule contract to fulfill *repetitive ordering for supplies or services* with the Contractor(s) that provide the best value. It is important to note that BPAs are *agreements not contracts.* This is a key distinction that has several important impacts. Simply put, it is much harder to enforce an agreement than a contract.

> **CO NOTE:** Also, FAR Part 8 BPAs are different from BPAs covered under FAR Part 13. We will discuss those under the Simplified Acquisition section.

The FAR also requires the CO to increase competition *"to the maximum extent practicable"* using multiple-award BPAs. The CO must document estimated quantities needed under the BPA, the amount of work to be performed, frequency of ordering, invoicing, discounts, time and locations for delivery.

FAR 8.405-3(b)(2) more specifically defines the procedures required for BPAs against FSS for services with a statement of work provided at hourly rates.

Federal Register Volume 77, Number 42 (pp. 12927-12929, Mar. 2, 2012) describes competition requirements for orders under multiple award BPAs. Those requirements include; a Request for

Quotation (RFQ) be sent to all BPA holders offering the required services for orders over the simplified acquisition threshold; all BPA holders be afforded an opportunity to submit a quote; all responses received be considered fairly; and the award be made in accordance with the selection procedures.

> **CO NOTE:** These conditions do not apply to BPAs awarded pursuant to part 13.

B. Simplified Acquisition Procedures (SAP)

FAR 13 mandates Agencies use Simplified Acquisition Procedures (SAP) for all acquisitions below the Simplified Acquisition Threshold (SAT), with a few exceptions. The SAT was $150,000 for most purchases at the writing of this book. See FAR 2.101 to see if it has been increased.

If the procurement is for a commercial item or service over the micro-purchase threshold (i.e., $2,500), then the procurement must follow the procedures in ***FAR Part 12***, Acquisition of Commercial Items. However, ***FAR 13.500*** may authorize using SAP if the procurement exceeds the SAT, but does not exceed $6,500,000. Although, there is a catch: this special authority is a Test Program expiring on January 1, 2015 (per ***FAR 13.5(d)***). COs must release the RFPs prior to expiration to use this Test Program authority. The good news is that with the exception of a brief window around 2008, this authority has been renewed every year for over a decade. Given the success of Agile techniques like this one, it is safe to be confident it will be renewed again.

Blanket Purchase Agreements under FAR Part 13

Another unique type of arrangement is the Blanket Purchase Agreement (BPA) as discussed in ***FAR 13.303.*** A **BPA** is a simplified method of filling anticipated repetitive needs for supplies or services by establishing "charge accounts" with qualified sources of supply.

FAR 13.003 states "Agencies shall use simplified acquisition procedures to the maximum extent practicable for all purchases of supplies or services not exceeding the simplified acquisition threshold".

BPAs may be either sole source or competitive. An agency can award multiple BPAs for the same supply/service. BPAs can be an efficient means to procure supplies and services, eliminating the terms and conditions of a "contract". A BPA is a written agreement of understanding and does not state or imply any agreement by the Government to place future orders with the contractor. Neither party can be held to continued performance under a BPA. BPAs can have a period of performance for up to five years. We have seen BPAs successfully used for things such as water delivery to remote sites where no potable water is available, golf cart maintenance, bottled water to be used by search and rescue teams, and bottled gases. Additionally, based on agency policy, the Government Purchase Card (GPC) can be used as a payment method on BPAs for transactions worth up to $25,000. This makes them very attractive to both the Government and agreement holder.

By establishing the terms of the agreement up front, with no guarantee of ordering (or delivering) the product or service, agency COs can use these BPAs to create an Agile network of pre-priced, pre-vetted vehicles to get goods and services quickly and at a reasonable price – with minimal administrative effort.

While designed for smaller purchases, the value of a BPA for creating an Agile procurement is that COs can use them for more complex goods and services provided the requirement is well defined. However, the trade-off is that because this is an agreement and not a contract, the CO does not have a "hammer" to force the contactor to comply. However, before using it, ask yourself, "Would you want to be the CO who awards a BPA to a company who is not actually capable of delivering?" Or ask yourself, "Would you want to be the contractor who had a BPA and told the CO, "No thanks" to a sale?"

SAP cannot be used to evade the requirements of the ***Competition in Contracting Act (CICA)*** so COs must promote competition with deadlines providing a reasonable opportunity for all interested Contractors to respond to the Government's solicitations. If the Government wishes to exclude any source(s), it must obtain prior approval using ***FAR Part 6*** procedures before the contract is issued.

The ***Federal Acquisition Streamlining Act of 1994*** (FASA) requires agencies to use commercial offerings whenever possible. However, before issuing a solicitation, they must make a determination, using market research, that appropriate commercial offerings are available, except for procurements under the micro-purchase threshold. The market research team builds a complete picture of competition in industry in order to understand if industry standard alternatives can offer the Government best value. The market research results must be published on the Federal Business Opportunities (FBO) website (www.fbo.gov). If the CO decides that commercial offerings cannot meet the Government's needs, that decision must be published in an FBO notice as well.

For complex procurements the market research team can:

(1) hold conferences about the proposed procurement with vendors, professional and trade organizations.
(2) attend trade shows and search web sites.
(3) contact others agencies who have recently procured similar items or services.
(4) distribute a Request for Information (RFI) via FBO.

FAR Part 12 procedures must be used for the procurement if the CO decides a commercial offer can fulfill the Government's need. Note that the introductory paragraphs of the ***FAR Part 7*** (Acquisition Planning) show the Government's clear preference for commercial, non-development items "to the maximum extent practicable" ***(FAR 7.102(a)(1)).*** Notice that FAR Part 12 Commercial Contracting is Agile because it builds on existing systems, processes and innovations – instead of trying to create new ones that the Government then has to manage afterwards.

The implementation of FAR Part 12 was a disruptive innovation initially (at least to the Government contracting world). Some agencies have overreached in their use of FAR Part 12.

> **CO NOTE:** To see an example of overreaching, Google "C-130J commercial item".

However, for the majority of goods and services, FAR Part 12 provides an outstanding opportunity to integrate Agile concepts and techniques. This is especially true when combined with ***FAR Part 13.5.***

FAR 13.106-1(b) states that only in situations where the requirements are urgent, or exclusive licensing already commits the procurement to a sole source, and the procurement is under the SAT, can the Contracting Officer ignore the SAP mandate for competition to the maximum extent practicable.

Competition should be promoted using electronic solicitations because an almost unlimited number of potential sources may respond to the Government's requirement. However, ***written solicitations*** including necessary drawings, blueprints, and specifications ***should be used for complex solicitations*** exceeding $2,000,000 such as in construction, to ***avoid requirements confusion.*** A similar parallel can be drawn to complex intangible systems, such as computer software, when requirements descriptions should include form, fit, and function to allow Contractors to propose alternative solutions giving the Government the best value.

CO's Perspective on SAP

FAR 13.002 states that the purpose of this part is to prescribe simplified acquisition procedures in order to:

(a) Reduce administrative costs;
(b) Improve opportunities for small, small disadvantaged, women-owned, veteran-owned, HUBZone, and service-disabled veteran-owned small business concerns to obtain a fair proportion of Government contracts;
(c) Promote efficiency and economy in contracting; and
(d) Avoid unnecessary burdens for agencies and contractors.

> **CO NOTE:** Consider the following related to the above:
>
> (a) Because "the contracting officer has broad discretion in fashioning suitable evaluation procedures", Government personnel do not have to spend as much time evaluating quotes or proposals for simplified acquisitions, thus reducing administrative costs.

(b) While this is well-intentioned, there is a strong and active (and some would say accelerating) trend to increase awards to all the various socio-economic groups. Therefore, with that trend in place already, one could argue that the SAP does not give these small businesses ***more*** of an advantage. They already have significant advantages and this simply builds on them.

(c) SAP promotes efficiency and economy by using a faster, more streamlined process. SAP can be done in under 6 weeks from start to finish (depending on the item or service being purchased). Compare this to complex, full source selections that can take up to 3 years to complete after all approvals and reviews are completed. The higher the contract value, the longer it takes to release the RFP, evaluate the proposals, and get approval to award.

(d) SAP definitely avoids burdens for the Government and contractors. Imagine having to submit a proposal with at least three volumes (price, technical, and past performance) along with any other documentation required, including a quality control plan, management plan, safety plan, etc. These routinely top 100 pages, and could exceed 5,000 pages.

Compare that to only submitting your catalog, commercial price list, specification, or fill out a simple quotation form. A proposal submitted under SAP is normally under 20 pages (some are under 10). For contractors, it is much easier and requires fewer resources to respond under SAP. For COs and Program Managers, it speeds up the competitive process and avoids 'documentation drills' that often plague larger source selections.

The risk with SAP is that it can be easy to misuse the process under the idea of 'speed'. Just because a CO ***can*** use SAP up to $6.5M for commercial items and services does not mean they ***should.*** Higher dollar, technically complex acquisitions may require detailed technical or management approaches, as well as successful past performance histories. There may be a need for some kind of tradeoff, which cannot be done when using SAP. By its nature, SAP is ***always Lowest Price Technically Acceptable (LPTA).*** So it behooves the CO to give some thought before automatically using SAP at the higher dollar levels permitted by FAR Part 13.5.

Simplified Acquisition Procedures can be a very Agile tool.

We have seen SAP used many times successfully. Some examples include hospital laboratory equipment maintenance, IT support, and athletic field maintenance. The key with each of these is that there are specific requirements any properly qualified contractor would know and be able to follow. Additionally, while they may total over $150,000, they are still relatively small dollar, non-complex requirements. There is no need for detailed technical evaluations or past performance history. By checking companies' System for Award Management (SAM) registration, the CO can see how long companies have been in business and which North American Industry Classification System (NAICS) codes they are registered under. Let's say the CO has a need for a five-year contract (one base year and four options) to buy IT admin support services. If the annual value is $200K, then over five years, this is $1M. By using FAR Part 13.5, the CO can still purchase these services using SAP.

...but it must be managed properly...

The examples of SAP not working well occurred when the PM and CO used poorly-developed specifications in the requirement. These poor specifications, after award, resulted in a contract that could not be performed for the proposed (and accepted) price. This is an example of the impact of poor up-front planning we discussed in the previous chapters.

However, this could (and does) happen regardless of whether the CO uses SAP or not. SAP, when used correctly, is a great tool in the CO's toolkit. Like any other tool, we have to know when to use a shovel and when to use a backhoe.

For other innovative and Agile techniques that are already available in the FAR, check out ***FAR Part 14***, Sealed Bidding. While sealed bidding sounds like (and has a reputation of) amplifying the worst parts of LPTA procurements, the reality can be quite different when used properly.

For example, two-step sealed bidding is already in the FAR, but very few people use it. Two-stepped Sealed Bid is essentially a two-step LPTA. However, the CO and PM conduct an evaluation of Technically Acceptability (Step 1) ***before the offerors even build their pricing proposal*** (Step 2). Some of the immediate benefits of this process include:

- CO saves ***hours*** of time evaluating sub-par proposals from offerors who cannot perform.
- Offerors avoid investing thousands of dollars in building and submitting a pricing proposal for work they cannot win.
- COs can trade that time saved to conduct better market research or to get feedback from offerors on what the specification should evaluate.
- Offerors can trade that time saved to spend more time targeting RFPs they are well-qualified to win.

This is a brief overview of the effective use of a Two-Step sealed bidding. See ***FAR Part 14.5*** or our visit blog at www.skywayacquisition.com/blog for more information.

C. Guidance on Choosing a Government Contract Type

The FAR requires COs to apply professional judgment when selecting the contract type to be used. Their objective should be to choose a contract type that will manage the Government's risk and motivate the Contractor to provide the most efficient and cost effective solution.

For complex, risky development programs, the Government has begun regulating contract type selection to avoid risking major litigation, which has occurred in the past after huge losses were incurred by Contractors in fixed price contracts.

FAR 16.000 and its subparts describe the various types of Government contracts used to purchase a large variety of supplies and services with the flexibility needed to purchase them in a vast array of quantities.

FAR 16.102 states that procurements using sealed bidding may only be awarded with FFP or Fixed Price with Economic Price Adjustment (FP-EPA) type contracts. Other unique nuances also apply, such as FAR Part 12 contracts that may only be awarded using FFP or FP-EPA. However, generally speaking, the CO has wide latitude to use any type, or combination of types, of contracts to promote the Government's best interest – and match the combination of market research, competitive circumstances to make the best business case.

Finally, contract type is only one part of the acquisition planning process (also known as the acquisition strategy).

> **CO NOTE:** A detailed explanation of the acquisition planning process is beyond the scope this book. For now, see FAR 7.105, or be patient because it will be covered in our next book that details the Agile techniques for Acquisition Planning.

> **"AGC NOTES":** The Generic Acquisition Model shown in Figure 1.2 could use a combination of Cost-type contracts. For example, it could use Cost Plus Fixed Fee (CPFF), Cost Plus Award Fee (CPAF), or Time and Material (T&M) contracts for Iterations 1 through 3, then award Firm Fixed Price (FFP), or Fixed Price Incentive Firm (FPIF) or even Fixed Price Award Fee (FPAF) contracts for Iterations 4 through N. When contracted this way, the first three Iterations are "pure" Agile, which is appropriate to the high-discovery nature of Value-Engineering and Risk Reduction. The remaining Iterations are a "hybrid" Agile approach using the series of Fixed Price contracts to help the Government retain the ability to stop a program anytime the cost / performance goals are not being met.

FAR 16.104 offers guidance the CO should consider during contract type selection, such as:

- Awarding a fixed price contract typically protects the Government's best interest by establishing a set price that can be relied upon to predict the most realistic pricing outcome. The risk of delivery falls squarely on the contractor.
- Careful and thorough price analysis increases the probability of realistic pricing, even in procurements where full and open competition is not possible, and can make a fixed price contract more appropriate.
- When price analysis cannot ensure a fair and reasonable price, then cost analysis, based on Government and Contractor estimates, factored for complexity, uncertainty and risk, should be used as the basis for contract type selection. In such situations, it is essential that reasonable responsibility for cost containment be placed on the Contractor.
- When complexity drives performance uncertainties or the probability of scope changes, it becomes more difficult to estimate costs in advance. Therefore, the Government must assume the majority of the risk and cost type contracts are appropriate. Also, as requirements' complexity increases, documentation of the risk assumed by the Government also needs to increase. However, as requirements stabilize or production begins and scales up, the cost-risk should be shifted to the Contractor using a fixed price contract.
- When time creates urgency becoming a primary driver of the procurement, the Government may need to assume responsibility for the risk of an accelerated schedule. Or, a contract with performance incentives may be needed to ensure timely completion by the Contractor.
- When the Contracting Officer has reason to question the Contractor's technical capability or financial capacity, it should be factored into contract type selection.
- When the Contracting Officer has reason to question the capability of a Contractor's accounting system, either a fixed price contract must be used or the accounting system must pass appropriate testing prior to using a cost-reimbursement type contract. Note: the accounting system can be assessed either by the Defense Contract Audit Agency, or by a Pre-Award survey that is normally conducted by the Defense Contract Management Agency.

D. Factors Impacting Choice of Contracting Vehicle

Beyond contract-type considerations, other factors impact the choice of contracting vehicle used. We will summarize them here, but we will not attempt to make the coverage exhaustive. If a detailed understanding is desired, the references to various FARs, DFARS, OMB Circulars, and Executive Orders can be consulted. And, of course, the LexisNexis' Federal Contract Management reference can be used for case law guidance.

You may also access the specific elements of the FAR ***(for free)*** at http://farsite.hill.af.mil. And don't forget to visit www.skywayacquisition.com for a free screencast on how to use the FAR Site tools.

1. Risk and Complexity

Uncertainty and complexity impact the work to be performed as part of the procurement and are a significant factor in selecting the correct contract type. As uncertainty and complexity increase, they increase the amount of risk involved to successfully deliver. Therefore, research and development, or similarly complex work being procured by the Government, should use cost reimbursement type contracts. At the other end of the continuum, production and similar predictable work should use fixed price type contracts. Basically, as risk rises due to uncertainty and complexity, work becomes more unpredictable and cannot be priced with reliability so cost-type contracts should be used.

Contract type is essentially about which party bears the risk of non-performance. The Government retains the risk of unsuccessful performance on cost type contacts. Fixed price contracts transfer the risk to the contractor. In simple terms, the profit (or fee) follows the risk. Whichever party has the risk, gets the majority of the profit (or loss).

For example, in ***Cost Plus Fixed Fee*** contracts, the profit rates can be as low as 0% or as high as 15%. Whatever the performance outcome, any savings accrue to the program and any overruns become the responsibility of the program to fund in order to complete the work. Often times this is necessary because no contractor will undertake the work without an exorbitant potential profit motive otherwise.

CO NOTE: In accordance with the ***Bona Fide Need Rule*** of fiscal law, any left over funds will "expire" if they are not used within a certain period. These funds are then transferred back to Congress to be distributed elsewhere. Congress no longer allows PMs and COs to keep the money they do not spend and use it in future years. Therefore, in an odd fact of Government procurement, the PMs are encouraged – and often mandated – to spend the funds they have before they go back to Congress on Sept 30th. There is much more to this of course, but this is the basic idea behind "expiring funds". You can find more details on the Skyway blog if desired.

For ***Fixed Price*** contracts, the profit can be as low as 0% or as high as 50%, depending on the good or service. In fixed-price contracts, the contractor bears all risk. Regardless of how much it actually costs to perform or deliver, the contractor will be paid the same fixed amount. Whatever is leftover (or not) is profit (or loss). The value and benefits of efficiencies now go to the contractor – in exchange for bearing the performance risk.

CO NOTE: When the CO ***competitively*** awards an FFP contract, the CO does not know – and is not entitled to know – the profit rate on the contract. Without competition, the CO still has to determine fair and reasonable price. Therefore, the contractors costs, rates, overhead, G&A, and profit must all be shared and agreed to by the CO. This is one of the fallacies of the efficiency of sole-source awards: they can create a whole additional documentation drill to validate the price without competition. In many cases, the contractor must also certify the accuracy of these costs if the contract is worth over $700,000. ***(see FAR 15.403-4).***

2. Profit

FAR 16.103 describes the concept of profit as an important factor in contract type selection. It states that both the Government and Contractor desire optimum performance by the Contractor, and identifies profit as the best incentive to stimulate outstanding performance. Therefore, the goal of contract type selection is to reward outstanding performance (and penalize poor performance) by aligning performance to profit rates using incentive-type contracts.

FAR Subpart 15.9 recommends policies for establishing pre-negotiation profit objectives. Similarly ***DFAR Subpart 215.9*** describes DoD policies and procedures for developing pre-negotiation profit objectives using cost analysis and the Weighted Guidelines Method.

The requirement for and the value of Weighted Guidelines.

In general terms, COs must use a structured approach to negotiating profit or fee when "adequate price competition" cannot be effectively used to validate a fair and reasonable price. The DoD's Weighted Guidelines Method is a profit assessment tool that is required when awarding non-competitive contracts worth more than $700,000 (per ***FAR 15.403-4(a)(1))*** to a for-profit company (per ***DFARS 215.404-4).*** The Weighted Guidelines method creates a useful starting point for COs (and savvy contractors) to begin negotiations by focusing on four profit factors: Performance Risk; Contract Type Risk; Facilities Capital Employed; and Cost Efficiency. The CO then assigns values to each factor based on the specific conditions of the requirement, company and business situation. In other words, the tool is standardized, but its use is customized to each situation.

The Weighted Guidelines Method is an existing Agile tool because the contracting officer can customize the factors based on the specific situation of each requirement and company. In addition, while it is required on specific contract negotiations, it is also a very useful tool for small, non-competitive contracts.

CO NOTE: There are different opinions on the effectiveness, accuracy and "fairness" of the Weighted Guidelines Method results. However, for the sake of this book, we recommend COs, PMs and contractors at least become familiar with it in order to use it to lead you through the Cone of Uncertainty.

E. Using a Termination for Convenience Clause

Cancellation of contracts when they are no longer needed, and for the reimbursement of costs actually incurred, is a formal Government policy supported by tradition, statute, and regulation. This termination policy permits flexibility in the face of rapid technological advances, shrinking budgetary allowances, and shifting priorities and political conditions.

This is also driven by the fact that the Legislative branch gives the money (or takes it away), and the Executive Branch spends it. So, if Congress decides to 'un-fund' something, the CO needs the ability to terminate the contract (since the CO cannot pay for it anymore).

Termination for convenience permits the Government to end a procurement contract without committing a "breach." Termination cancels the Contractor's obligation to deliver completed supplies or further services under the terminated portion of the contract.

The standard "termination for convenience" ("T4C") clauses in a Government contract provide the instrument for broad Government rights whenever it learns that termination is in its best interest. It also limits a Contractor's recovery of costs incurred to payment for completed work, and the cost of preparing a termination settlement proposal. They often preclude recovery of anticipated profits, when a FAR-version termination-for-convenience clause is incorporated, unless the Contractor can show that the Government acted in bad faith or abused its discretion in invoking the termination clause.

CO NOTE: The standard T4C clauses include:

52.249-1 - Termination for Convenience of the Government (Fixed-Price) (Short Form)

52.249-2 - Termination for Convenience of the Government (Fixed-Price).

52.249-3 - Termination for Convenience of the Government (Dismantling, Demolition, or Removal of Improvements).

52.249-4 - Termination for Convenience of the Government (Services) (Short Form).

52.249-5 - Termination for Convenience of the Government (Educational and Other Nonprofit Institutions).

52.249-6 - Termination (Cost-Reimbursement).

52.249-7 - Termination (Fixed-Price Architect-Engineer).

Terminations for the Government's convenience allow almost total discretion to act in its own interest, for its own "convenience," to terminate a contract according to the contract clause in the absence of bad faith or clear abuse of the Contracting Officer's discretion.

FAR Parts 12, 13, 31, and ***49*** define requirements for termination and settlement of Government contracts. Most commonly, COs will use these FAR Part 49 clauses for terminations. For contract award under commercial procedures, COs will use the termination procedures in clauses 52.212-4.

FAR 52.249-2 also provides that the Government may terminate performance of work under a fixed price contract in whole or, from time to time, in part, if the CO determines that the termination is in the Government's interest.

These clauses give the CO the fullest discretion to end the contract in the sole interest of the Government. This discretion may be exercised to minimize a bad bargain or improve a contractual position by buying elsewhere at a cheaper price. Under the current budget constraints, it is just as likely that a contract may be "T4C'd" due to lack of funding to continue the work.

CICA, which requires full and open competition, supports the position that it is not an abuse of discretion if the facts support a reasonable inference that the CO terminated for convenience in furtherance of the statutory requirements for full and open competition.

Typically only prior bad faith conduct will subsequently prevent the Government from benefitting from terminating for convenience.

Termination may be complete, ending all of the work that has not been completed and accepted, or it may be ***partial***, ending some but not all of the incomplete work. ***Partial termination eliminates identifiable work items***, reduces the number of units to be delivered or reduces contract tasks.

A breach of contract by the Government causes the relinquishment of its right to invoke termination for convenience. A breach of contract includes any failure, without legal excuse, to perform any promise that forms the whole or part of a contract.

To be binding, the notice that its contract is being terminated for the Government's convenience must be in writing. Failure to follow the requirements for a T4C (per ***FAR 49.102(a)***) can subject the Government to a breach of contract lawsuit. The written T4C notice must state:

(1) The contract is "terminated for the convenience of the Government" and identify the contract provisions authorizing such termination;

(2) The effective date of termination;

(3) The extent of the termination;

(4) Any special instructions; and the steps the contractor should take to minimize the impact on personnel if the termination, together with all other outstanding terminations, will result in a significant reduction in the contractor's work force.

CHAPTER

6

Contracting Procedures

Since this book serves as a field guide, our purpose in this Chapter is to describe a variety of specific, step-by-step procedural outlines that Department, Command and Agency Leaders, Contracting Officers, Procurement Professionals, Program Managers, and Prime and Sub-Contractors can engage in Agile Government contracting.

Each proposed process has been researched, engineered, and designed to comply with all the relevant regulatory standards and save the user – ***YOU*** – hundreds of hours of research and analysis, that would otherwise be necessary to support negotiating, planning and delivering desirable outcomes on procurements and programs of all sizes.

Each description is intended to be instructive, ***not*** exhaustive. It avoids theoretical debates that, although interesting and hold merit, do not focus on practical, useful, concrete processes for moving forward.

As you already know, the Government can utilize sealed bidding and negotiation / competitive proposals for many acquisitions. However, sealed bidding is rarely used in Federal Government contracting any more due to the push for "tradeoffs", which cannot be supported under this methodology. Remember, in Chapter 5 we described the case for using 2-step sealed bidding in lieu of LPTA. There are also other procedures that can be applied to specific categories of procurements differing from those standard Government processes, creating an Agile procurement.

We will focus on those specific differences and provide a working knowledge of options and process ideas that can be applied.

Then, when a detailed application of the process is desired, the various references to FARs, DFARS, OMB Circulars, and Executive Orders can be consulted for guidance.

A. The Source Selection Procedure

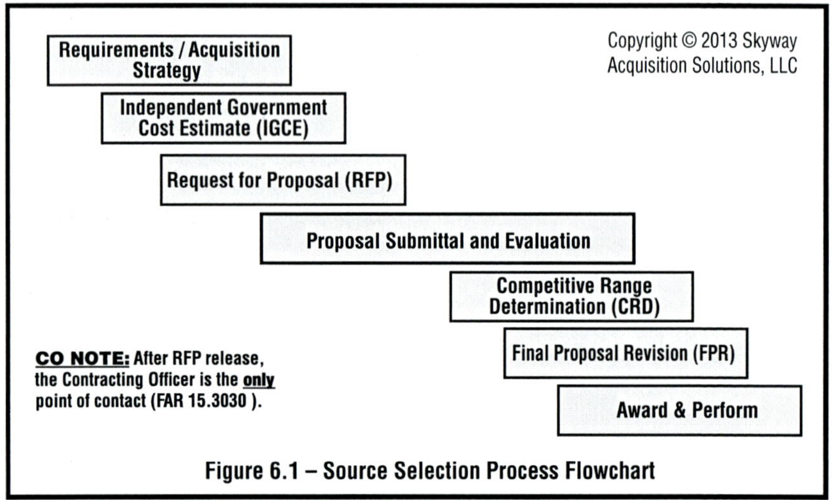

Figure 6.1 – Source Selection Process Flowchart

This section is an overview of the source selection process. Because this is meant to be instructive, not exhaustive, there are many specific steps we either under-emphasized or skipped altogether. For specifics on the source selection process, see ***FAR Part 15*** and ***DFARS 215.*** This chapter is designed to provide only a wave-top understanding.

We also acknowledge, again, the potential divide between DoD and civilian agencies and the need for caution when suggesting DoD practices might apply to civilian agencies. This section supports DoD procurements, but has strong parallels in source selection for federal civilian agencies. It if does not apply to your situation, please feel free to disregard or reach out to the authors for further consultation.

Requirement and Acquisition Strategy

Requirement: The first steps in any acquisition are to (a) define the requirement and (b) find the best acquisition strategy to buy the product or service. While this may sound simple, it is not. Simply defining the specific requirement to a level of detail that the CO can procure is usually a daunting effort. The user (or end customer) and the PM need to invest the necessary time and knowledge to clearly define what they want. This detail is then pressed into a Statement of Work (SOW) from which the CO can build an acquisition strategy.

Acquisition Strategy: There are thousands of Federal and Defense Department policies that the CO and PM need to consider here. For example: Competitive or sole source? Small business or other socio-economic set-aside? Commercial or non-commercial? Are there mandatory sources for the item/service?

The process begins with market research (requests for information or source sought synopsis) and meetings with industry. The CO needs to ensure the customer actually knows what they need (see paragraph above). For example, if the requirement is a new x-ray machine, should the CO buy it, or would leasing it be more cost efficient? Does the customer need a maintenance plan? If the contract does not include maintenance, does the Government have organic personnel to perform this? Is it available on Federal Supply Schedules?

Bottom line: The requirement identification and acquisition strategy are not on a single path. It can be more like a winding road as the team travels through the Cone of Uncertainty before determining the "minimum needs of the Government" and the "best value acquisition approach".

Independent Government Cost Estimate (IGCE):

During the market research phase, the customer needs to prepare an Independent Government Cost Estimate (IGCE). This is a complex process because it is critical that the IGCE be as accurate as possible. The days of taking the current contract price and escalating it by 3.5% and calling that the IGCE are gone. Careful thought needs to go into this estimate. It will come under scrutiny throughout the entire review process and needs to be realistic and meaningful. This is where the interaction between the CO and industry are so crucial. The more robust the interaction between them, the more realistic the IGCE will turn out.

Request for Proposal (RFP)

Once the market research and IGCE are complete, the CO can put together a Request for Proposal (RFP). A strong specification will ensure the right item or service are procured. To begin, the team must develop appropriate evaluation criteria to ensure the contract will be awarded to a contractor who can perform the work. It must include all the required acceptance criteria and terms and conditions that will ultimately become part of the contract. The evaluation criteria are normally those elements most important to the User. For example, is the ability to deliver quickly the most important factor? Is price? Is the amount of experience the key factor in choosing a successful contractor? The best RFPs clearly show what the Government team is expecting to receive - and how they will evaluate it.

Proposal Submittal and Evaluation

Submitting and receiving proposals is the next step. This process has its own set of challenges. Did everyone submit proposals by the required time? Did they provide all the requested information? The evaluation team can range from a few technical experts and the contracting team may include dozens of additional people, depending on the dollar value and complexity of the requirement. Every proposal will be evaluated for technical acceptability, fairness and reasonableness of the price, and any other factors included in the evaluation criteria from the RFP. The success of each step in this process builds on the clarity of the last step.

Competitive Range Determination (CRD)

Determining the competitive range is normally only used in larger source selections (over $1M). However, it is a worthwhile step in the process, even with smaller value contracts. Establishing a CRD can be difficult, especially when several offers are all technically acceptable and have roughly equivalent pricing. In many cases, proposals will have outliers that are clearly too low or too high and can be eliminated. However, this is not always the case.

In recent years, the preference has been to keep all the technically acceptable offers within the competitive range to help drive up competition and give everyone a "fair chance." The logic is that this limits the need for post-award debriefing of those that did not make it into the CR and may reduce the possibility of a protest.

However, with an Agile approach, it is much better to eliminate companies who have very low odds of winning. Agile principles suggest, if they do not have a good chance to win, they are wasting their time continuing to develop their response and the CO's time evaluating it. Eliminating waste is a key principle of Agile and this is an obvious opportunity to apply it. Therefore, we recommend that the CO limit the CR to only those companies who have a strong chance of winning.

Final Proposal Revision (FPR)

When offerors are included in the CR, the CO provides a list of improvements or Evaluation Notices (ENs) that the offerors can address to improve their chance of winning. Each offeror's response to being in the CR is their Final Proposal Revision (FPR). The FPR is also based on any amendments made to the RFP and those clarifications are shared with all potential offerors as the result of the discussions. This FPR is the final adjustment to their proposal, accommodating any revisions to the RFP and responding to the ENs.

Contract Award

The contract award process is a lot more complicated than these few pages allow, but it is the next step. Absent any protests or other issues delaying performance, contract award indicates the CO (and PM) believe they have found the best way to get their customer what they need at the best possible price.

Of course, now performance has to be monitored. This is called the "Post Award Phase" or Contract Administration. That part of the process can be just as challenging as making the award decision in the first place. However, that content is outside the scope of this book, but planned for our next one. If you have thoughts about or interest in Contract Administration, please feel free to reach out to the authors.

B. Time and Materials and Labor-Hour Contracts

Time and Materials (T&M) contracts are the simplest to adapt to an Agile procurement, so we will begin there.

FAR 16.601 and ***16.602*** cover T&M contract types used to procure supplies or services based on direct labor hours paid at specific, pre-negotiated hourly rates (that include profit), typically including overhead burden and material reimbursement at cost.

> **"AGC" Notes:** The reason Time and Material contracts are the easiest to use is because the Government retains the ability to stop the procurement anytime the cost / performance goals are not being met. For example, in the Generic Acquisition Model shown in Figure 1.2, at any point in the high-discovery Value-Engineering and Risk Reduction phase, if an economically untenable obstacle occurs that cannot be overcome, the program stops. Likewise, during the Construction Iterations, if an economically untenable problem arises, the Government is not obligated beyond the current Iteration.

The problem with this contract type for the Government is that the Contractor's profit motive runs counter to controlling costs. Therefore, it is best to only use T&M contracts when reliable price or cost estimates are ***not*** possible. Most often this is the case where the final deliverables of the procurement must be developed in an environment of high-complexity and high-uncertainty.

The *T&M Labor Hour contract* is a variation where the Contractor does not supply materials.

Most often these contract types are used when the deliverable from the procurement is intangible, such as software, engineering designs or planning, or where the procurement includes a significant majority of intangible content.

FAR 16.601(d)(1) requires the CO "prepare a determination that no other contract type is suitable", has made use of these contract types very rarely, and are an almost "last resort" choice.

In fact, T&M is currently such an unpopular type of contract, most agencies require specific approvals to use T&M or LH contracts. For example, Special Operations Command requires that, for all T&M contracts over $1M in one year, the CO write a Determination and Findings (D&F) that must be approved by the SOCOM Director of Procurement. The D&F must explain why a T&M or LH contract is the only viable option for contract type.

> **CO NOTE:** Having to write an additional document to explain the decision is not Agile strategy.

Therefore, T&M is not recommended very often. A Cost-Plus Fixed Fee (CPFF) may be a better option because it allows for some of the flexibility of T&M, but does not allow the contractor to attach profit directly to labor hours. The profit (or fee) is a fixed amount based on a pre-established amount of work. See the section on CPFF later in this book.

The key to protecting the Government's interest in a procurement using this type of contract is to:

(a) Define requirements and any technical trade-offs that will impact usage and operating and support costs, as specific evaluation criteria, or metrics.
(b) Set specific cut-off dates for each Iteration, and Release, to deliver working features or functionality to be evaluated.
(c) Publish the procedures used to evaluate technical or system performance of deliverables at the end of each Iteration or Release.
(d) Contract for procurement and include a Termination for Convenience clause in contract.
(e) Complete Iterations 1 through N, subject to a successful evaluation of each prior Iteration's deliverables.
(f) Complete a detailed evaluation at the end of each Iteration, comparing the deliverables against the defined evaluation criteria and make a Go / No-Go decision before committing to or funding the next Iteration.
(g) If a No-Go decision is made, exercise the Termination for Convenience clause.

Figure 6.2 shows the flow of procurement activities when a T&M contract with a Termination for Convenience clause is used.

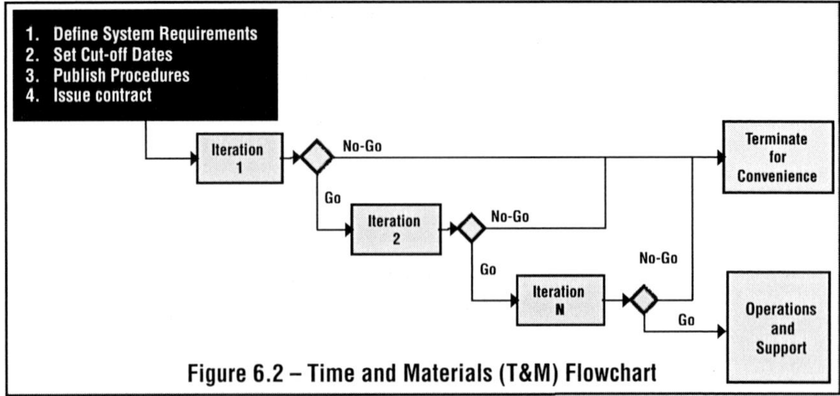

Figure 6.2 – Time and Materials (T&M) Flowchart

The procurement can be delivered as a series of interlinked Iterations. Iterations can be grouped into Releases, if desired. As the program progresses, the CO and PM must stay in close communication so contractual controls are exercised in alignment with developmental progress.

C. Multiple Award Contracts (MACs)

FAR 16.504(c) explains the preference for MACs, which are a type of IDIQ contract. MACs are awarded to several (multiple) firms from a single solicitation. They are not multiple awards to various offerors for the development of different concepts, technical approaches, or prototypes leading to the selection of one approach. They are also not split awards in which a definitive requirement is divided by line item or lot among various offerors.

"AGC" NOTES: The reason MACs are highly functional is because the Government can use a single solicitation to identify multiple, potential Contractors then execute the procurement in Iterations. For example, in the Generic Acquisition Model shown in Figure 1.2, any of the Iteration awards could be given to any of the eligible Contractors in the MAC. Or, the Government could issue two solicitations – one for the Value-Engineering and Risk Reduction Iterations and another for the Construction Iterations – then issue two MACs. Either way, the Government can protect itself from being obligated beyond the current Iteration and continue to make decisions based on cost / performance data.

Whenever an IDIQ contract is appropriate, there is a preference for the use of MAC procedures. During acquisition planning, the CO must determine whether MACs are appropriate.

IDIQ contracts have become a preferred Government contract type because of their administrative convenience and improved pricing. However, serious misuse and mismanagement has occurred in several key areas including; requirements that are so broad, they are meaningless and unenforceable, or mediocre performance and large pass-through costs from specialized Sub-Contractors.

FAR 52.215-22 and **52.215-23** provides guidance on management of Pass-through Costs.

To avoid those and other pitfalls, MACs must contain an appropriate SOW and/or a specification forming the basis for a mutually binding contract when the initial contract is awarded. That condition is important because it means when a MAC order is placed, work can begin without delays due to pre-contract impediments.

MACs balance the benefits of creating robust competition with well-defined requirements against the need for streamlined procurement processes. They avoid the long administrative lead-times needed to negotiate individual definitive contracts, while limiting the cost/performance uncertainties of traditional indefinite-delivery contracts due to broadly defined requirements in the solicitation.

Clearly framing requirements drives source selection to the best value services.

MACs can be particularly valuable in eliminating the deficiencies related to ***professional services contracting*** because they ensure the Government knows its specific requirements at the time of order placement. ***Clearly framing requirements drives source selection to the best value services.*** MACs use the initial competition to select an appropriate number of competent sources with differing strengths that can be applied to specific requirements of specific orders. The MAC prequalification technique drives the benefits of competition without the delays that would occur if each order were competed as a separate contract. In principle, this technique combines the administrative convenience of indefinite-delivery contracts with the precision and clarity of definitive contracts.

D. Indefinite-Delivery Contracts

The Government utilizes three types of indefinite-delivery contracts.

- ***FAR 16.502 – Indefinite-Delivery, Definite-Quantity***
- ***FAR 16.503 – Indefinite-Delivery-Requirements***
- ***FAR 16.504 – Indefinite-Delivery, Indefinite-Quantity (IDIQ)***

These contract types are utilized when the Government cannot identify the exact time and/or quantity of future deliveries when the contract award is made.

FAR 16.502 explains that Definite-quantity contracts procure specific supplies or services during a specific or fixed period. Typically, deliveries are scheduled to locations specified when the order is placed.

FAR 16.503 explains that Indefinite-Delivery-Requirements contracts procure specific supplies or services when the Government places orders with the Contractor. The CO must include realistic estimated quantities, based on the most current information available regarding Government requirements, of the various supplies or services in the solicitation and resulting contract. However, those estimates are not a commitment to purchase.

This type of contract may be appropriate for recurring services where the Government anticipates a need, but cannot predetermine the precise quantities during a specific period.

FAR 16.503(a) states that a Requirements contract is awarded to one Contractor and overrides any implication in ***FAR 16.503(b)(2)*** that it may be awarded to multiple sources.

FAR 16.503(a)(l) compels the Government, when it adjusts its estimates due to changes in funding priorities or other reasons, to notify offerors of those adjustments or be held liable to compensate the Contractor for any shortfall in orders.

FAR 16.504 explains that IDIQ contracts procure an indefinite quantity of specific supplies or services, within stated limits, during a defined period. The contract requires the Government to order the stated minimum, and not to exceed a stated maximum quantity, of the specific supplies or services. The CO's statement of the maximum quantity must be based on the most current information available.

The Government only funds the stated minimum quantity at the time of contract award, providing additional funds when an order is placed. Unless the Government issues a written order under the IDIQ contract, there is no implied contract. When the Government places an order, delivery is scheduled.

"AGC" NOTES: ***A Definite-Quantity*** contract can be ***used for services*** that are readily available during the contract period. To use this approach, maintenance, computer programming, or other services could be defined as Hourly-Units delivered to a virtual or physical location. Each type of Hourly-Unit would be assigned a specific cost, with higher costs when more expertise is required and lower cost when not. The Definite-Quantity would be set at the funding limit or some lesser amount.

This approach would be used when the quantity of services desired and the specific timeframe for their delivery were both known.

Using this contracting vehicle, the CO could coordinate with the Program Manager to authorize batches of those Units to provide the specific deliverables within the approved time period.

"AGC" Notes: An ***Indefinite-Delivery-Requirements contract*** can be used to arrange for anticipated service needs before the exact demand is known without making a commitment until the needs are known.

For Agile Government Contracting, this type of IDIQ contract can be used to arrange for specific minimum quantities of services before the exact demand is known. The only commitment is to the minimum quantity.

Again, to use this approach, maintenance, computer programming, or other services could be defined as Hourly-Units that are delivered to a virtual or physical location. Each type of Hourly-Unit would be assigned a specific cost, with higher costs when more expertise is required and lower cost when not.

The Indefinite-Quantity would be based on the CO's estimates or on contract minimums. Using this contracting vehicle, the CO could coordinate with the Program Manager to authorize batches of those Units to provide the specific deliverables within the approved time period.

E. Alpha Contracting aka Teaming on Proposals (TOPs)

Alpha Contracting is primarily an Agile strategy when awarding a contract on a sole-source basis (see ***FAR 6.3*** for the conditions under which to do so). Alpha Contracting ***relies on a team approach*** in a procurement process using a concurrent exchange of information from solicitation development through proposal preparation, evaluation, negotiation, and award, to meet customer and supplier objectives. It allows major system requirements, as well as subsystems and components, to be under contract in months, rather than years.

Successful Alpha Contracting relies on the ability of the Government and Contractor to operate as a team throughout the contract formation process. Team members must focus on solutions benefitting all parties. By uniting as a team, the Government and Contractor focus on efficient development and reduced pricing by identifying and eliminating unnecessary or unaffordable elements of scope prior to proposal development. This process maximizes delivery of program requirements within program funding limits. Thus, the Government obtains best value in a much shorter time frame.

Alpha Contracting ***avoids*** the typical sole-source procurement cycle where first, the program office goes through a repetitive process of multiple internal drafts and reviews to define requirements, often with limited understanding of manufacturing constraints or technical advances that could benefit them. This is then followed by months of effort in the procurement office to incorporate the requirements into an RFP. A second repetitive process begins, where the Contractor creates detailed Work Breakdown Structures (WBS) and other schedules to address each element of the RFP, with a primary focus on strict compliance rather than alternatives that could reduce program costs, speed delivery times and improve results. Next, a third repetitive process involves the Contractor creating drafts and holding internal reviews until the formal, often multi-volume proposal is sent to the CO, initiating yet another repetitive review cycle as the Government team begins its lengthy evaluations. And, there is always the risk of the Government's evaluation launching a final repetitive process requesting supporting information where necessary changes to requirements are discovered, possibly returning the whole process to the beginning.

While that description may sound almost comical, the results are anything but funny! The process drives costs higher, increases risk as time is lost, and any collegial esprit de corps has been extinguished.

Alpha Contracting implements many of the concepts in the pre-award phase of the DoD's ***Integrated Product and Process Development (IPPD)*** approach using an integrated team to established a contract best meeting the needs of the End User. Participants in Alpha Contracting include the Customer, the Buying Command and CO, the Program Office and Program Manager, and Defense Contract Management Agency (DCMA) and Defense Contract Audit Agency (DCAA) auditors as well as key Users, the Prime Contractor and principal Sub-Contractors.

Successful Alpha Contracting requires a core team of committed, seasoned professionals capable of understanding and negotiating each element of the program, then selling each aspect of the final agreement within their individual organizations.

To achieve the desired outcome, Alpha Contracting requires appropriate delegation of authority to the core Alpha Team members so they can bind their individual organizations to the agreements made during the process. Within the boundaries of each member's fiduciary responsibility to their respective employers, the parties negotiate in the best interests of the program. The Alpha Contracting process creates transparent communication so each party clearly understands the overall requirements and how they individually contribute to fulfilling defined mutual objectives.

Also critical to Alpha Contracting success, is empowering the core Alpha Team members to limit participation to individuals who can review, discuss, and ultimately accept or reject specific cost estimates. Without decision-making power, expensive time will be spent and bid and proposal costs, on both sides of the table, will increase.

The team develops integrated requirements as a baseline for jointly defining technical and cost details that will go into the contract. During the process, the team identifies ways to provide better performance or lower risk and cost by changing the baseline or how to integrate the baseline components. Jointly, the team develops an approach with an affordable and achievable scope that improves performance and quality by eliminating non-value-added components of the program scope.

The output of the team's effort is a model contract with optimized program requirements, instead of an RFP. If Government pricing and audit personnel were included as the technical details were shaped, the end result can be a fully negotiated, supported contract. This approach usually does not produce a traditional solicitation or proposal, instead resulting in a contract, typically with a lower overall cost than originally anticipated.

As Figure 6.3 shows, Alpha Contracting begins with a basic Government-developed scope of work and specifications. Then, the team chooses a contract approach, formulates a general high-level WBS, and develops a rough-cut target schedule and cost. Next, they develop a model contract, complete with a preliminary scope, contract line item structure, schedule, and terms and conditions.

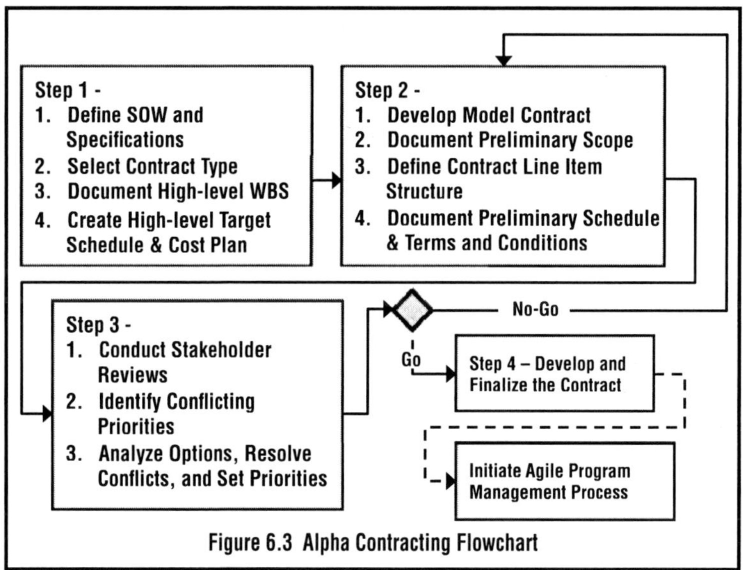

Figure 6.3 Alpha Contracting Flowchart

Working from that common set of initial data, the team develops a thorough understanding of each organization's positions and works to eliminate conflicting priorities thereby reducing costs. The team reviews and discusses each program element searching for formal agreement on how to proceed. Additionally, estimators work to forecast the cost changes associated with specific scope changes, aiding the team in identifying useful trade-offs.

As program elements are developed and agreed upon, price and cost negotiations are documented in memoranda, leading to a final, fully priced agreement.

In the end, both the buyer and seller obtain a thorough understanding of the program scope and cost of fulfillment. By jointly developing the program scope and pricing, the probability of future disagreements on requirements or cost assumptions is greatly reduced. In turn, that lowers program risk because expectations have been aligned with an achievable, executable program plan and fewer post-award modifications. The final outcome represents the best opportunity for the seller to meet the buyer's objectives.

An additional, indirect benefit of the open communication model is that it reduces the Contractor's potential liability for inadvertently failing to disclose current, complete and accurate cost and pricing data. See ***FAR 15.4***, Contract Pricing and ***FAR Part 42,*** Contract Administration and Audit Services for more information on these pricing specifics.

During the 1990s, many agencies implemented the Integrated Product Team (IPT) approach. The team would remain permanent throughout the contract acquisition cycle and consist of all the personnel needed to take a contract from pre-award to post-award. The team included, at a minimum, the CO, the contract specialist, a pricing analyst, engineers and other technical representatives. The concept was that the team all sat together, collocated, rather than remotely located in different buildings so the probability of increased team creativity and synergy would occur. And in some cases, it did.

This idea of collocating core team members is the preferred best practice in Agile Project Management today.

CO NOTE: Kevin worked in an IPT procuring training systems, including trainer aircraft and simulators for the Air Force B1-B Training Simulator. It was very effective having the entire team within reach to talk through issues and ideas. It removed stovepipes and created an environment of trust. They all knew each other's role and why they had to communicate needs and concerns effectively.

While the IPT concept worked well, it became difficult to maintain fixed teams that did not allow personnel to work on a variety of projects. When downsizing occurred, it became impossible to continue the practice of having a dedicated team for each contract.

A more current version of this type of process is the multi-functional team (MFT) used for service acquisitions. All the stakeholders become part of the MFT and work on the requirement from definition to market research, technical evaluation development to evaluation, contract award through performance and eventual closeout. This team is broader than the IPT was, as it includes the same members mentioned above, as well as a procurement analyst, a legal advisor, a finance/accounting member, and other advisors as needed.

The MFT meets periodically over the course of the acquisition, allowing them to do other work also. With the broader range of team members, combined with the flexibility for the members to work on other projects, the MFT process has been more viable than the IPT.

Some agencies still use the IPT approach today, but acknowledge it has disadvantages too. One is that the COs are separated from other COs – creating a knowledge vacuum because peers are not sharing in each others learning and creativity. This is can be offset through technology, but is not a perfect replacement. Collaborative tools such as Sharepoint and Lessons Learned workshops, allow the COs to maintain their internal and external camaraderie.

F. Modular Contracting

Modular Contracting is a procurement method reducing the inherent risk in the traditional, grand-design-mode information technology acquisitions of the past, where systems were often extremely expensive, missing desired capabilities, and outdated when delivered because they were years behind schedule.

To function properly, the traditional procurement model must have predictive precision for planning, funding, and acquisition. That is extremely difficult – impossible really – to achieve for technology procurements. Technology acquisitions must deal with changing technical and User working environments driving the high-magnitude complexities and risks involved in large-scale development. Experience has shown that the rigidity of the traditional model actually induces risks and mistakes instead of minimizing them.

The Modular Contracting model, on the other hand, leverages the opportunity to adapt to the realities of the IT environment and apply them to the procurement. By decomposing delivery, implementation, and testing of the system into discrete increments, each module can be acquired with a single- or multiple-procurement contract. Legally, the Government is only obligated to purchase one module at a time.

Using Modular Contracting, a Department, Command or Agency, directly or through its Prime Contractor, incrementally awards work and manages program progress based on factual information of work completed. It makes informed decisions centered on demonstrated, working pieces of the solution rather than on estimates, projections, and forecasts.

The ***Clinger-Cohen Act*** (Pub. L No. 104-106, 1996) states that major IT system procurements can be subdivided into several smaller acquisitions and done in increments or modules. It suggests this approach because smaller, incremental acquisitions are easier to manage than a single, comprehensive procurement and because there is a higher probability of delivering useful workable solutions. Finally, it describes an approach where delivery, implementation, and testing of workable systems or solutions occurs in discrete increments not dependent on future procurements to provide important functionality and the opportunity to leverage future acquisitions takes advantage of technology's continuous evolution to higher power and lower cost.

As Figure 6.4 shows, the probability of success diminishes for projects that are too rushed or too prolonged. There is a correct amount of time for project execution. As a general rule, shorter projects have a higher probability of success. Therefore, a series of shorter projects has a higher probability of success than a single, longer project pursuing the same goals.

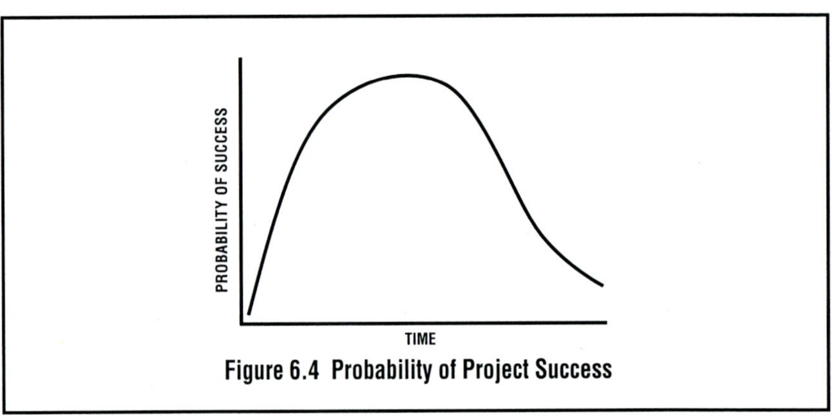

Figure 6.4 Probability of Project Success

The Modular Contracting process starts with defining system features and functions, then moves into developing the architectural and engineering structure so that a viability assessment can be done. That assessment leads to a Go/No-Go decision. If a decision is made to proceed, the program planning process is executed and development Iterations are started. As Iterations are completed, a decision to Deploy or Hold is then made, followed by a decision on whether the project is done or not. Figure 6.5 shows the flow of the Modular Contracting process.

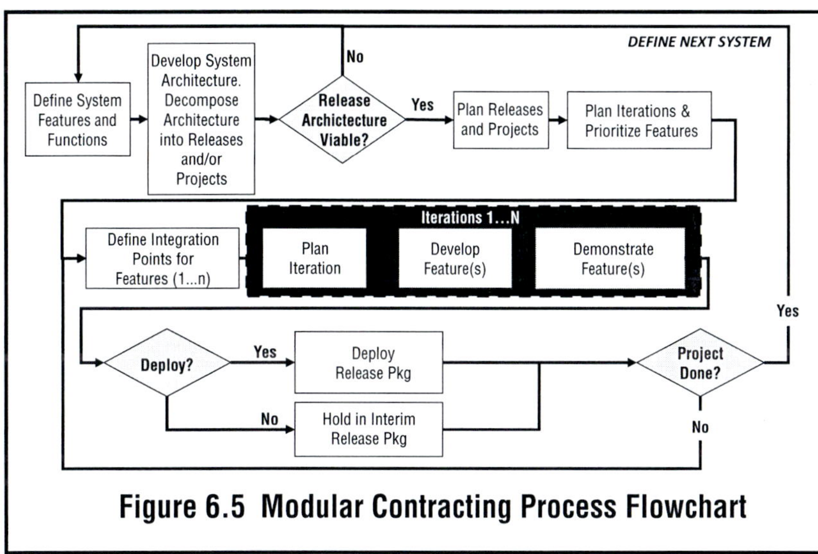

Figure 6.5 Modular Contracting Process Flowchart

> **CO NOTE:** For Agile Government Contracting it is worth noting that Modular Contracting is, perhaps, the closest facsimile of the Agile frameworks used extensively in the commercial and industrial marketplaces.

Modular Contracting guidance comes in legislative, policy, regulatory, and budgetary categories. Let's look at them.

FAR 2.101 has defined major systems as any system designated by the head of the agency responsible for that system. That definition combined with the Clinger-Cohen Act creates a pretty broad field for applying Modular Contracting.

OMB Circular A-109, Major Systems Acquisition, expresses guidance aligned with the Clinger-Cohen Act and focused on procuring major systems using an integrated approach.

OMB Memorandum 97-02, Funding Information Systems Investments, established decision criteria paralleling Modular Contracting and is often referred to as Raines Rules. The criteria define specific situations where the OMB will or will not recommend new or continued funding investments in major IT systems.

Those criteria support Modular Contracting with a preference for systems being implemented in narrowly scoped increments using Iterations that are as short as practicable. The goal is to resolve a specific mission problem while delivering measurable benefits not dependent on future procurements.

OMB Circular A-11, Planning, Budgeting and Acquisition of Fixed Assets (Part 3), provides specific budgeting guidance for using a modular approach.

By coupling Modular Contracting with Task Orders priced for a single module based on the final design review, both pricing and schedules become more realistic. At the same time, the agency retains flexibility because they can revisit cost, technical, and schedule assumptions against actual progress.

> **"AGC" NOTES:** Task Orders can be issued for each Iteration, and acceptance and approval for payment can be aligned with the deliverables demonstrated at the end of the Iteration.

As stated in the Clinger-Cohen Act, agencies must decide whether the procurement can be decomposed into apparent, logical segments in order to determine whether Modular contracting is practicable. The concept of a module can vary significantly from program to program.

> **CO NOTE:** In practice, the CO should require the development of an initial, high-level system design so that the practicality of identifying logical breakout points, or interfaces, can be determined.

In many cases, the Department, Command or Agency and CO may need the services of a systems integrator to assist with the initial, high-level system design. Then, if the system is a candidate for

Modular Contracting, the CO and Program Manager can develop a module breakout structure and decide the phasing of each module. Using a system design this way will create a better understanding of needs and constraints, define realistic system deliverables, and reduce down-stream risk with more informed decisions and contracting up-front.

The system design also enables solution development where each module is independent of subsequent modules for important functions, and where required agency IT standards are maintained, thereby reducing integration risk.

While some modules may be dependent on other modules in order to be fully operational, typically a functionally-acceptable degree of interoperability can be defined to facilitate development while minimizing integration risk and enabling practical Modular Contracting.

Selecting the appropriate Modular Contracting procurement approach is an important key to success. After determining requirements, constraints, and contingencies, the system design the Department, Command or Agency chooses must balance the benefits of competition against the risk of different Contractors developing modules.

The contract should be structured so each module is procured independently and the Agency is not required to purchase additional modules. The procurement and contract must also comply with the time requirements (i.e., thresholds) defined in the Clinger-Cohen Act. That means the contract, "to the maximum extent practicable," be awarded within 180 days of the solicitation issue date, and scheduled for delivery within eighteen months of the solicitation (i.e., within twelve months after contract award). Those requirements suggest an IDIQ contract with Task Orders as a likely vehicle to support the CO using Modular Contracting as a procurement approach.

Traditional procurements share two risks; cost overruns and long schedule overruns, both of which are often caused by ***unclear performance objectives.*** Modular Contracting helps, but does not guarantee, the CO will avoid the risks posed by unclear performance objectives. Only diligence can guarantee avoiding unclear performance objectives. Modular Contracting also introduces new risks that must be managed.

The chief risk raised by Modular Contracting is integration. Failure to manage the integration risk significantly raises the risk that independently developed modules will have flaws or gaps resulting in system failure.

Modular Contracting must address responsibility for, and the process of, system integration as the Government decomposes the system into successive procurements of interoperable modules. Because the Government rarely has the internal expertise to manage system integration, in most cases, an outside Contractor should provide support.

> **"AGC" NOTES:** One approach is to have a Prime Contractor be responsible for system integration and, perhaps, production support for an initial period following deployment, but not actually build the system. Instead, the Prime Contractor manages the build by defining the design, architecture and interfaces, and using Sub-Contractors to build it.
>
> This approach has the added value of creating long-term stability because of a continuing, structured relationship with the Prime Contractor that would not exist if each module were awarded to a different Contractor.

Another risk, at a more tactical level, is managing and prioritizing system requirements. If the Department, Command or Agency commits prematurely, it can limit the system design to an unwise choice, adversely affecting the final system. To mitigate this risk, COs and Program Managers must jointly adopt effective reporting and monitoring procedures for both module-specific and system-wide reviews. Those reviews must include key Department, Command or Agency personnel and all Contractors.

G. Basic Ordering Agreement

FAR 16.703 explains that a Basic Ordering Agreement (BOA) is a procurement tool, not a contract. It is an agreement that describes the prices to be paid for supplies or services during the specified period of the BOA. Authorized personnel issue binding orders in strict compliance with the terms specified in the BOA. However, a BOA does not imply a Government obligation to place any orders.

The Government uses BOAs because they reduce administrative cost and time. However, to use a BOA, and prior to placing an order, the CO must determine that using sealed bids or competitive proposals is impracticable. Un-priced orders can be placed using a BOA, but must follow specific guidelines.

> **"AGC" NOTES:** BOAs may be integrated with other approaches in order to maximize flexibility.

H. Leader Company Contracting

In ***FAR Subpart 17.4,*** Leader Company Contracting describes having a developer or sole source provider, known as the Leader Company, furnish assistance and know-how, enabling another company, known as the Follower Company, to become a supplier of an item or system.

This is a special type of Government procurement with a primary focus on ensuring future competitive procurements by eliminating the need for sole source contracts. It may also be designed to accomplish other objectives, such as shortening delivery time, creating additional sources of supply or supporting the transition from the development environment to economically desirable production volumes.

> **"AGC" NOTES:** Leader Company Contracting may be integrated with other approaches, such as treating the Prime Contractor as the Leader Company and the various Sub-Contractors as the Follower Company, in order to maximize long-term flexibility.

Leader Company Contracting is only used when the Government finds the Leader Company is the only source of supply for a specific Government requirement and the Leader Company assistance is limited to what is vital to enable the Follower Company to produce the items. The Government must approve the contract between the Leader Company and the Follower Company.

There are various approaches to using a Leader Company procedure. One choice is for the Government to require the Leader Company to assist the Follower Company via a subcontract for a specific portion of end items. A second choice is for the Government to contract the Leader Company to furnish specific assistance required by the Follower Company, enabling them to qualify as a producer of the item or the system.

CHAPTER

7

Other Transactions (OTs)

In 1989, the Defense Advanced Research Projects Agency (DARPA) received Congressional authorization, later extended to the DoD, to use a procurement approach known as Other Transactions (OTs) to emulate commercial processes and increase efficiency. By definition, OTs are anything other than grants, cooperative agreements, or contracts.

In 1994, the ***DoD National Authorization Act, Section 845*** expanded the OT authorization from development projects, with both military and civilian applications, to include acquiring exclusively military prototypes. Since prototypes were not defined by the regulations or in case law, broad application of Section 845 has occurred.

We will cover two specific types of application. ***Section 845*** Other Transactions: ***Prototype Acquisition Authority*** and ***Technology Investment Agreements.***

A. Section 845 OTs: Prototype Acquisition Authority

Under the DoD National Authorization Act, Section 845, ***even in situations where a standard procurement contract is appropriate and feasible,*** the DoD is allowed to experiment with OTs. The Section 845 authority seeks to streamline acquisitions, eliminating the requirement for cost sharing. It includes the power to use non-FAR contracts for procuring prototype deliverables, but ***not*** production deliverables.

The statutory requirement limits Section 845 projects to those directly relevant to "weapons or weapon systems", which can include subsystems, components, and technologies.

> **"AGC" NOTES:** The language is broad enough to include training, simulation, and other types of support and equipment.

The Section 845 authority creates opportunities for innovation for both Traditional defense Contractors and non-Traditional companies because of its broad ability to adopt commercial best practices. Even though agreements may appear to be Government contracts, by most definitions, they are not subject to the FAR or the ***DoD Grant and Agreement Regulations (DoDGARs).***

Section 845 includes a statutory requirement that prototype projects be conducted with competition to the maximum extent practicable. Therefore, any time a CO initiates a Section 845 project without competition, a well-documented rationale should exist.

Competition for Section 845 prototype projects should be clear to address statutory testing requirements while avoiding non-value-added activities.

FAR 6.102(b) and ***FAR Part 15*** provide competition models that can be used in prototype projects. Another approach is to follow ***FAR 6.102(d)(2)*** and ***FAR 35.016*** and use the Broad Agency Announcement (BAA) technique.

> **"AGC" NOTES:** Entirely new forms of competition are created with proposals and oral presentations being combined and customized for special circumstances.

Competition for Section 845 prototype projects should also address alternatives to Traditional Government-developed SOWs. One best practice is to use a series of incremental progress goals aligned to an affordability goal.

With Section 845 OTs, the initial solicitation is typically used to determine the capability of various Contractors to design, architect or engineer a prototype design. During proposal evaluation, multiple competing Contractor teams are selected and multiple awards, in equal amounts of seed money, are made to begin Phase 1.

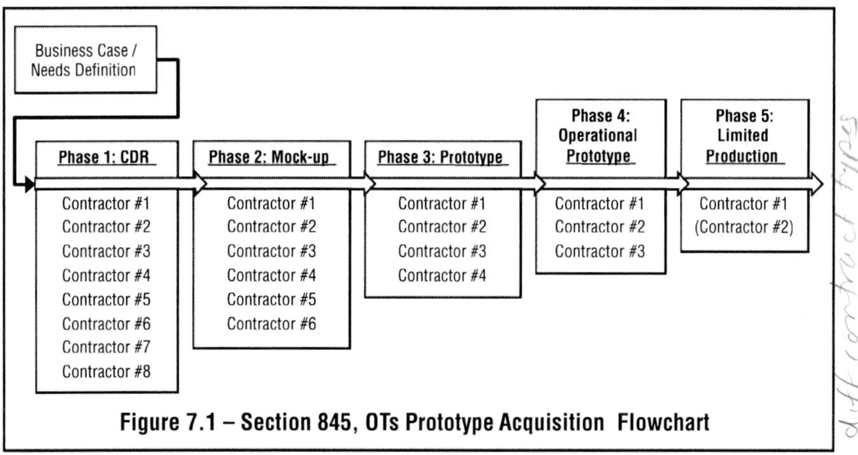

Figure 7.1 – Section 845, OTs Prototype Acquisition Flowchart

In Phase 1, Contractors develop competing conceptual, preliminary designs. Each preliminary design requires performance and cost tradeoffs needing validation. Therefore, a milestone-driven schedule to produce the needed validation, and associated payments, is carefully defined during the negotiation. The Contractor teams may include specialized Sub-Contractors in their teaming arrangements. Often, Contractor cost exceeds the amount paid by the Government in this phase, creating a shared-risk relationship. The successful Contractor teams are selected because they offer the most desirable performance profile within the cost goal.

Phase 2 involves developing critical designs, components, and subsystems, sometimes including fabrication of mock-ups and initial testing. The goal is to establish expectations regarding performance to cost tradeoffs within the absolute cost limit. At the end of Phase 2, there is another down-select to Contractors with the most promising performance profiles within the cost goal. Cost-Plus-Incentive-Fee (CPIF) contracts are usually used.

In Phase 3, fabrication of prototypes occurs and, after appropriate field-testing, needed changes and upgrades drive planning for prototype modifications. It also includes another down-select to the Contractors with the most promising performance profiles within the cost goal. Again, most often, CPIF contracts are used.

Phase 4 normally involves developing operational prototypes and a final down-select to the Contractor or Contractors with the most promising performance profiles within the cost goal. Usually Fixed-Price-Incentive-Fee (FPIF) contracts are used in this phase.

In Phase 5, the successful Contractor or Contractors produce limited-production quantities at target prices. Contracts are typically FFP.

Throughout the process, the Contractor, who confers with the Government representative in a collaborative relationship, controls product design details.

B. Technology Investment Agreements (TIAs)

Technology Investment Agreements (TIAs) can be utilized when the mutual interest of the Government and the Contractor are aligned or balanced. When both parties have specific needs and the deliverables will fulfill both, such as developing a technology like the Global Positioning System (GPS) that can be used by the Government to enhance its military mission and the Contractor to make a profit from consumer products, a TIA is a sound choice.

Guidance published by the ***Director of Defense Research and Engineering (DDR&E)***, now known as the ***Assistant Secretary of Defense for Research and Engineering (ASD (R&E))***, states that TIAs can be used to stimulate or support a program where the Contractor has an inherent interest in the work and not just in making a profit.

Model TIAs have also been used by Departments, Commands and Agencies for dual-use programs where the Contractor is actually an industry consortium.

Along the way, many lessons have been learned about effectively using TIAs. We will cover four of them here.

1. Using Milestones Payments

Because most commercial relationships are based on fixed payments for specific measurable performance or deliverables, many TIAs pay agreed-upon fixed amounts for completion of milestones, not costs incurred. This requires the Government to clearly describe milestones and acceptance criteria so that if the milestone is not completed correctly, payment can be denied. When contracted this way, the milestones operate like a series of fixed-price agreements.

2. Using Commercial Accounting Methods

Many TIAs agree to let the Contractors, who are not regular defense Contractors with systems already certified under Government cost accounting standards, use Generally Accepted Accounting Principles (GAAP) rather than the cost principles in the FAR and DFARS. This is acceptable because the mandatory strict labor reporting requirements, such as for cost-reimbursement contracts, do not apply to fixed-price milestones.

Collecting data and reporting on labor-hours is a program management tool for determining how much effort is being expended and how much progress is being made. Therefore, because Government cost principles may not be selected to control TIAs, Contractors' employees are permitted to report their chargeable hours weekly, or even monthly, depending upon company policy.

3. Managing TIAs

Under the DARPA model, a TIA program has scheduled, periodic reviews where decisions on milestone payments are made. These reviews may require additional investigations that may or may not occur during the scheduled ones.

The scheduled reviews are joint sessions where Government Program Managers and the Contractor, or alternately, the consortium members, work as peers and partners to assess progress and plan future activities.

Because TIAs typically cover complex work with high uncertainty, the team recognizes, anticipates and even invites changes that enhance program results.

4. Ensuring Requirements Flowdown

The typical flowdown of Government contract terms and conditions does not apply to TIAs, with two important exceptions subject to negotiation. The first exception is that Research and Development (R&D) procurements must include flowdown clauses protecting the Government's patent and data rights and also preventing technology transfer to foreign firms, institutions or Governments without prior approval. The second exception is that TIAs are not subject to the ***Buy American Act and Trade Agreements Act*** of 1979 unless specifically required in the appropriation and Sub-Contractors' certifications of compliance with laws, such as Equal Employment Opportunity, are not required.

CHAPTER

8

Accounting Control and Progress Reports

Earned Value Management (EVM) has been in use since the 1960s in Traditional Project Management environments, particularly on defense and construction projects. EVM is a widely recognized program management technique included in the Project Management Institute, *A Guide to the Project Management Body of Knowledge, (PMBOK® Guide) – Fifth Edition, Project Management Institute, Inc. 2012*. EVM is also recognized by many other organizations including the American National Standards Institute (ANSI), the International Performance Management Council (IPMC) and the Advancement of Cost Engineering International (AACE).

In this section, EVM will be covered only briefly because it has been discussed by a great many authors elsewhere. We will explain it here as a bridge to understanding its application in Agile procurements.

Earned Value Management (EVM) is a Program Management technique that integrates scope, schedule, and resource consumption information in order to measure project performance against planned cost metrics. It provides quantitative, objective data to supplement qualitative, subjective judgments.

For COs and Program Managers, using EVM to report against a cost baseline supports fulfillment of their responsibility to prevent misdirected development, careless resource usage, and unauthorized changes. Once a committed Iteration plan has been defined, a cost baseline can be documented and approved. Knowing it will be necessary to do so improves both Government and Contractor discipline in planning and contracting.

Using that information provides needed visibility so any contract changes can be negotiated and authorized within the scope of the contract.

A. Earned Value Management (EVM)

EVM is an important part of any Agile procurement because APM frameworks do ***not*** articulate how to identify, track and manage costs. APM frameworks do ***not*** include a cost or budgeting process or tool.

As a Program Management tool integrating the technical, cost, and schedule parameters of a contract, EVM enables Agile procurements to fully function in Government environments.

In Agile procurements, the ideal level to manage the cost baseline is the Iteration. EVM work measurement would typically be at the end of the Iteration, but it could be associated with specific Features or Stories at a lower, more granular level.

For most organizations, managing it at the Release level is not granular enough despite being less costly. Once the cost/benefit ratio is understood, most organizations set standards for Iteration length reporting because it provides the needed granularity and also controls the cost of reporting.

One best practice is to analyze variances and formally evaluate them on an end-of-Iteration basis, even if the cost information is captured and recorded at a lower, more granular level.

EVM's fundamental premise is that as work is completed, the corresponding budget value is earned, and that paradigm aligns at the most basic level with APM. Agile frameworks can measure completed work at the Story, Feature or Iteration level and EVM calculations can be applied.

Although EVM can be applied to many Agile elements, in order to implement EVM effectively, the organization must decide how much reporting detail is required because as the need for more detailed, granular, reporting increases, the time, effort and cost required to produce it increases as well.

CO NOTE: EVM is great tool when used properly. Like many of the tools in this book, the CO and PM must consider the time, cost and impact of having contractors implement the EVM systems on each program. In addition, the acquisition team may need some training on EVM to ensure they understand the meaning of the data in each category (BCWP, PV, ACWP, AC, CPR, IMS, etc.)

As a note of caution, Kevin has only seen EVM used successfully on large contracts (over $500M).

The CO and PM must use sound judgment and discretion to balance the benefits EVM provides against the cost associated with setting the initial planning values, oversight, management, and training required to properly manage it.

Remember, the Agile goal is to eliminate waste!

B. Progress Reporting

Beyond the use of Agile's basic charts and reports, there are many more standard and customizable reporting options available with EVM. Because progress is measured and reported as completed units – Stories, Features, or Iterations – EVM charts share significant similarities with Agile charts and reports. The contribution that Agile makes is simply better, more reliable data. And that is a contribution that should not be overlooked!

"AGC" NOTES: For Agile Government Contracting to actually be possible, it will be necessary for COs and Program Managers to become skilled in using similar new tools and processes. While that is not an inconsequential challenge, there are many reports the Agile Project Leader can use to promote a value-oriented perspective within the Department, Command or Agency team as well as within Contractor teams.

Delivering Actionable Reports

The best recognized reports in Agile are referred to as "Burn-down" and "Burn-up" charts. The power of these simple charts lies in the clarity with which they articulate the project's two most important numbers – ***how much work remains*** and the ***net-net rate of progress*** – against the project scope including all changes and challenges.

Burn-down charts show the work ***remaining,*** like number of story points or ideal days left to be completed. They are used most often for Iterations and typically reflect the results of the team's daily meeting.

Burn-up charts show the work ***completed***, typically in story points or ideal days, for the Project or Release. These typically reflect Features or Deliverables completed.

Burn charts are rarely smooth because they reflect the team's actual progress. Because of breakthroughs or unexpected technical challenges, estimate variances, and scope changes, a Burn-down chart may show negative progress where the line of progress goes up instead of down during an Iteration. Such a line radiates insight that the work the team has completed is not occurring at the expected pace. In other words, the team's "net-net" progress suggests a threat to completion of the entire project scope.

The value of a Burn-down chart is directly proportional to the length of the Iteration. Because the value of the chart comes from seeing trend lines and adjusting the development approach when needed, the shorter the Iteration, the smaller the value of the Burn-down chart. With very short Iterations, by the time a trend is recognizable it is too late to adjust.

The standard Iteration Burn-down chart is two-dimensional. It plots time on the horizontal X-axis and work remaining on the vertical Y-axis, as shown in Figure 8.1.

The two most common ways to create and manage a Burn-down chart are manually, for co-located teams, and using Excel for remote, distributed teams. The most common mistake made on Burn-down charts is overcomplicating the process. A Burn-down typically reports the sum of all work remaining, on a daily basis.

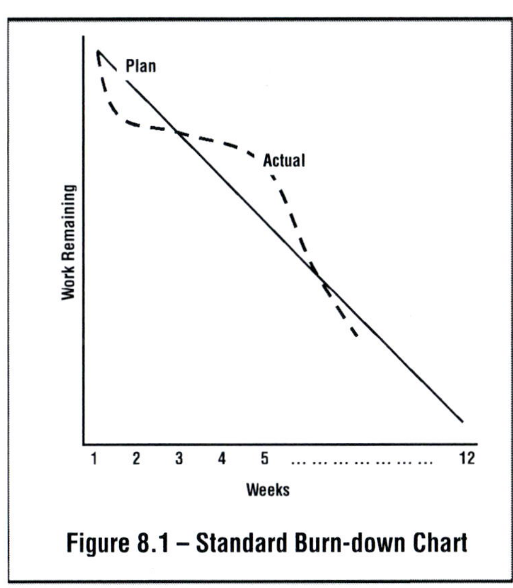

Figure 8.1 – Standard Burn-down Chart

Based on the team's status updates, changes to the data are recorded, so the work remaining is accurately plotted on the chart. If the team identifies additional tasks or unexpected difficulty and therefore estimates additional work time is needed, the increase will be reflected on the chart. Conversely, if they experience a breakthrough, substantially decreasing the estimate of work remaining, the decrease will be reflected on the chart.

The emerging trend line becomes a powerful visual communicator of the team's progress towards the Iteration goal.

Figure 8.2 shows a combined Burn-up and EVM chart where the information is plotted as four lines. The Agile Baseline, which is equivalent to the EVM Planned Value, runs diagonally from the lower left to the upper right. Then the line for Stories Completed is shown rising as each Story is completed. For this example, we assumed that value was only earned when a Feature was complete, and we defined each Feature as being composed of four Stories. So the Earned Value line rises in a stair-step pattern after the four Stories in each Feature are completed. Last is the Actual Cost line, which rises faster than the other lines until story completion and earned value catch up. The final point recorded shows that Stories completed and EV have intersected above the cost line so Earned Value exceeds Actual Cost.

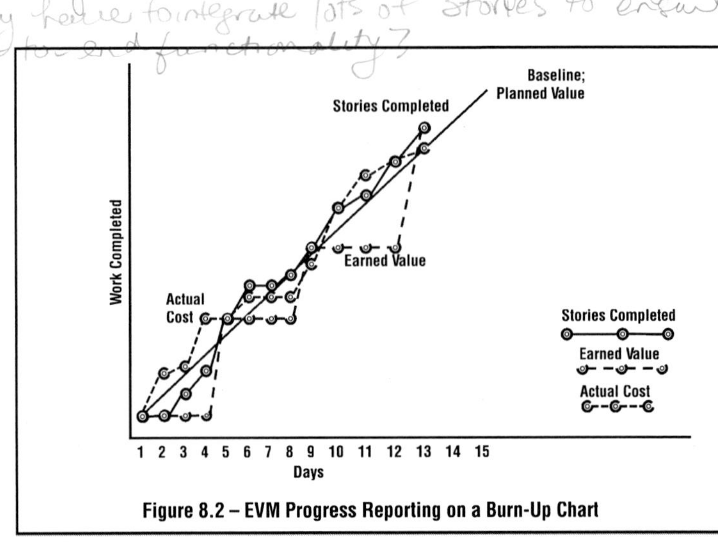

Figure 8.2 – EVM Progress Reporting on a Burn-Up Chart

Using Burn charts implies the existence of a Feature, Story or Task Board – typically a physical one for co-located teams or an electronic one for remote, distributed and virtual teams.

C. EVM and Feature, Story and Task Boards

All the various Boards used in APM contain a collection of cards describing Features, Stories or Tasks that include the relative size or estimate of effort. Both pieces of information – ***what to do*** and ***how big is it*** – are critical because they are used to determine the best approach for solution development and how to manage it.

Feature Boards are a collection of cards describing Features with a high-level of granularity and long time horizons.

Story Boards are a collection of cards describing Stories with enough detail to support effective Iteration planning.

Task Boards are a collection of cards describing the Tasks that must be completed in order to deliver the committed Stories for the Iteration goal.

The detail granularity increases as Features are decomposed into Stories and Stories are decomposed into Tasks. The team uses Story and Task Boards during their daily meetings to focus discussion on the topics needed to synchronize their work efforts. They also provide a convenient, visual radiator of the project's work organization as well as how much work is left. In a sense, it is a narrative explaining the quantitative results shown on the burn chart.

Because the primary duty of the Task Board is enabling team synchronization, it must be designed with the flexibility to allow self-organization of their work. As the project progresses, many Tasks and Stories are in the backlog and typically not assigned to specific individuals. When a team member finishes a Task, they select a specific Task to do next. Typically, they explain their planned choice so other team members can express concurrence, concern, or make alternate suggestions until a mutually agreeable decision is made. By being easily visible and flexible, the Task Board helps the team see which Tasks are being worked and which are available to choose.

Task Boards can be corkboards, whiteboards, flipcharts, walls, windows, cubicle dividers or even the backs of files cabinets with columns delineated using masking tape. The central design element of the Task Board is the column. Columns define the process steps or development stages that Tasks or Stories pass through from backlog to completion. The Tasks or Stories are written on sticky notes or cards and are fixed, taped or pinned in a column, starting in the Backlog column.

Then they move, in Western convention, from left to right as they progress towards completion. If they encounter difficulties, they can be moved in the opposite direction and return to a prior process step for rework. Many enhancements can be added to the basic card convention, including color-coded cards to signify specific feature groups or priorities, sizing or estimate information, and prioritization information.

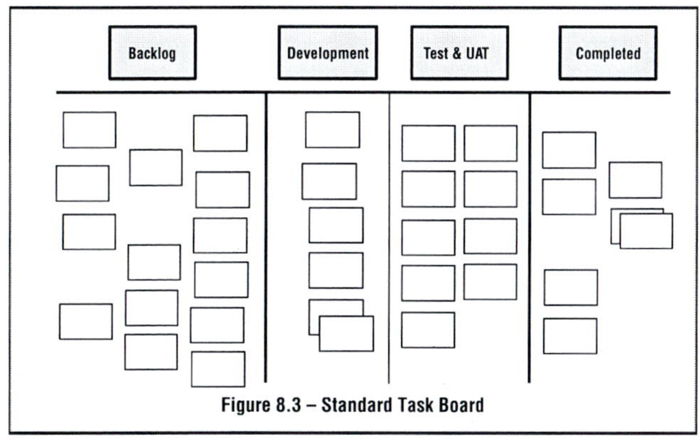

Figure 8.3 – Standard Task Board

Figure 8.3 shows a task board with columns for Backlog, Development, Test & UAT, and Completed. For this team and project, those were selected as the categories needed to enable proper synchronization and self-organized planning. They also represent a continuum of progress that the average stakeholder can decipher to understand the state of the project and correlate it to the burn chart usually displayed nearby.

Beyond the use of Agile's basic Burn-Up chart, there are many more standard and customizable reporting options available with EVM. The contribution that Agile makes is simply better, more reliable data. And again, that is a contribution that should not be overlooked!

APPENDIX

A

Acronyms

APM – Agile Project Management

ASD (R&E) – Assistant Secretary of Defense for Research and Engineering

BAA – Broad Agency Announcement

BOA – Basic Ordering Agreement

BPA – Blanket Purchase Agreement(s)

CBD – Commerce Business Daily

CDC – Center for Disease Control

CDD – Capability Development Document

CICA – Competition in Contracting Act

CPIF – Cost-Plus-Incentive-Fee

CPFF – Cost Plus Fixed Fee

CSM – Certified Scrum Master

CSP – Certified Scrum Professional

DARPA – Defense Advanced Research Projects Agency

DCAA – Defense Contract Audit Agency

DCF – Discounted Cash Flow

DCMA – Defense Contract Management Agency

DDR&E – Director of Defense Research and Engineering

DFARS – Defense FAR Supplement

DHS – Department of Homeland Security

DoD – Department of Defense

DoDD – DoD Directive

DoDGARs – DoD Grant and Agreement Regulations

DoDI – DoD Instruction

EPLC – Enterprise Performance Life Cycle

ERP – Enterprise Resource Planning

EVM – Earned Value Management

FAC-P/PM – Federal Acquisition Certification for Program and Project Managers

FAR – Federal Acquisition Regulations

FASA – Federal Acquisition Streamlining Act

FBS – Feature Breakdown Structure

FFP – Firm Fixed Price

FMR – Financial Management Regulation

FP-EPA – Fixed Price with Economic Price Adjustment

FPIF – Fixed-Price-Incentive-Fee

FSS – Federal Supply Schedules(s)

GAAP – Generally Accepted Accounting Principles

GSA – General Services Administration

GWACS – Government-wide Agency Contracts

HHS – Department of Health and Human Services

HHSAR – Department of Health and Human Services' Acquisition Regulation

HSAM – Homeland Security Acquisition Manual

ICD – Initial Capability Document

IFB – Invitations for Bids

IOC – Initial Operational Capability

IDIQ – Indefinite-Delivery, Indefinite-Quantity

IPPD – Integrated Product and Process Development

ITIL – Information Technology Infrastructure Library

JCIDS – Joint Capabilities Integration and Development System

MAC – Multiple Award Contract(s)

MAS/FSS – Multiple Award Schedules / Federal Supply Schedule

MDA – Milestone Decision Authorities

MMF – Minimal Marketable Features

NASA – National Aeronautics and Space Administration

OMB – Office of Management and Budget

OTs – Other Transactions

PMI – Project Management Institute

PMP – Project Management Professional

PMI-ACP – PMI-Agile Certified Practitioner

R&D – Research and Development

RFI – Request for Information

RFP – Request for Proposal

RFQ – Request for Quotation

ROI – Return on Investment

ROM – Rough Order of Magnitude

SAP – Simplified Acquisition Procedures

SAT – Simplified Acquisition Threshold

SOW – Statement of Work

T&M – Time and Materials

TCO – Total Cost of Ownership

TIAs – Technology Investment Agreements

VAR – Value-Added Reseller(s)

WBS – Work Breakdown Structure